# Learning Language Arts Through Literature

THE GOLD

TEACHER BOOK

*British Literature*

By

Greg Strayer, Ph.D.

and

Timothy Nichols

*See where learning takes you.*

The *Learning Language Arts Through Literature* Series:

*The Blue Book* - 1st Grade Skills
*The Red Book* - 2nd Grade Skills
*The Yellow Book* - 3rd Grade Skills
*The Orange Book* - 4th Grade Skills
*The Purple Book* - 5th Grade Skills
*The Tan Book* - 6th Grade Skills
*The Green Book* - 7th-8th Grade Skills
*The Gray Book* - 8th-9th Grade Skills
*The Gold Book American Literature* - High School Skills
*The Gold Book British Literature* - High School Skills



**Common Sense Press**
8786 Highway 21
P.O. Box 1365
Melrose, FL 32666
(352) 475-5757
*www.commonsensepress.com*



Printed in the United States of America.
Rev 06/03
ISBN 1-929683-11-1

# Introduction

*The Gold Book-British Literature* is written in a style that provides instructions and directions for the student and teacher in an easy-to-use format. Thought provoking questions and answers guide the student and teacher into learning experiences filled with opportunities for critical thinking and analysis. We highly value the teacher's opportunity to help shape and develop the student's understanding and beliefs, so we encourage discussion on issues raised in literature. The poems and novels examined in this manual have been selected to demonstrate literary principles. The authors of these selections are considered among the best and most influential of British authors. Upon consideration of these authors, please note that these authors and their works are secular. While their works are not religious in nature, the topics they consider raise questions that can and should be answered out of the context of faith.

We suggest that the teacher read over the literature and the questions to determine if any content or questions may be of concern. We do not necessarily recommend the other literature selections in the collections of poems and encourage the teacher to evaluate them prior to having them read by the student.

*Learning Language Arts Through Literature, The Gold Book-British Literature* is written as a college preparation course that may be used at any high school level. We are pleased to present this excellent manual for teacher and student.

# How to Use This Book

*The Gold Book-British Literature* is designed to be used by the student and the teacher.

Each lesson consists of a five-day week, complete with assignments and questions. *Answers* are located at the end of most lessons for easy reference. Many of the questions are designed to be interactive and may be answered orally or as a written assignment. We encourage the teacher to vary requirements for oral or written answers depending on what will best assist the student in learning. Be sure to spend some time discussing the answers. We also suggest adjusting reading assignments to meet the student's needs. If the student requires more time to read a novel, the lessons may be adjusted accordingly.

We suggest the student keep a notebook divided into four sections:

1) Section One: record any written answers to questions
2) Section Two: journal writing (Lessons 4-5)
3) Section Three: poetry writing
4) Section Four: writing assignments and book reviews (Or if the student uses the computer, this section may be used for brainstorming, outlines, rough drafts, etc.)

When a literary term is introduced, it will be highlighted in bold print, followed by its definition. The list of literary terms is provided at the back of this manual.

In conclusion, we hope this language arts course will encourage the high school student's ability to read and understand literature as well as develop the ability for verbal and written expression. It is also our desire that the student be able to interpret and assess literary meaning in terms of content and philosophy, and then be able to clearly state a position in response. As the student's understanding of literature grows, it is our prayer that there will be equal growth in the ability to "give an account for the hope that is within you."

To complete the assignments in this manual, the student will need the following books:

*Frankenstein, or, The Modern Prometheus*, by Mary Shelley, published by Bantam Books ISBN 0-553-21247-8 (or any edition of the 1818 publication)

*Emma*, by Jane Austen, published by Bantam Books ISBN 0-553-21273-7

*A Tale of Two Cities*, by Charles Dickens, published by Penguin Group ISBN 0-14-043054-7

*The Time Machine*, by H.G. Wells (any unabridged publication)

*Animal Farm*, by George Orwell (any unabridged publication)

*The Mentor Book of Major British Poets*, edited by Oscar Williams, published by Penguin Group ISBN 0-451-62637-0

## Table of Contents

# An Emphasis on Poetry

[1] rhyme: the repetition of similar sounding syllables, usually at the end of lines
[2] meter: the rhythmic pattern of stressed and unstressed syllables

1. a. Learning from the Past

When I taught the poetic technique classes to junior college students, I rarely had a student who knew anything about the craft of writing poetry. Unfortunately, almost all of them thought they knew everything about poety. Therefore, I would have to spend the first two weeks unteaching them and stripping away their mistaken notions, before I could actually teach them anything of substance. I couldn't just lay down some rules, however, without explanation. The students needed to know why their understanding of poetic technique was in error. To accomplish this, I spent a little time explaining that the form and content of poetry reflects the culture from which it is derived.

For example, the Greeks of the Hellenistic period saw the world as being in a rather chaotic state. They felt it was necessary to bring order to their unstable environment through an orderly thought process that they called reason. Their temples, sculptures, and even their dramas were created with mathematical guidelines in order to reflect perfection. In their minds, poetic form had to have a regular metric pattern, a regular number of syllables per line, etc. This concept of poetry-that a regular and measured form is necessary-derives from the Greek tradition in Western civilization. This preoccupation with ordered language in Western culture probably reached its height during the Enlightenment, often called the Age of Reason.

The Age of Enlightenment is generally considered to begin with the publication of Isaac Newton's *Mathematical Principles of Natural Philosophy (Philosophiae Naturalis Principia Mathematica)* in 1687, and to end with the onset of the French Revolution in 1789. During this period, rules for proper poetic form were carried out to an extreme. Such excesses reflected the scientific and philosophical thought of the Enlightenment. Consequently, when the basis for the principles of the Enlightenment changed, so did the form and content of poetry; therefore, today, such conventions as rhyme[1] and **meter**[2] are no longer obligatory, but have their proper place as resources which the poet is free to use, or not to use, as he pleases.

Newton's discovery of the universal law of gravitation provided evidence of a growing belief that our surroundings could be understood by careful observation, experimentation, and mathematical and rational analysis. Newton calculated the force of gravitation, then projected that this force was the same for all the heavenly bodies. Thus, using Newton's formula, the force of attraction between the moon and the earth, earth and sun, etc. could be calculated. Newton's universal law of gravitation was proof to many that everything in our experience operates by the forces of natural laws. Such laws must govern all phases of our existence, it was thought, and were not confined to just mathematics and physics. Thus, shortly after Newton's publication of the *Mathematical Principles of Natural Philosophy*, there followed John Locke's natural laws for government and Adam Smith's natural laws for economics. It was inevitable that literature would reflect this scientific and philosophical revolution.

Alexander Pope (1688-1744) was the leading poet of the Enlightenment, and a great admirer of Isaac Newton. Pope was well acquainted with the philosophy of his time and this was reflected in the form, subject matter, and diction[3] of his poetry. Since Pope set the example, others followed, and poetry of the Enlightenment had very distinct characteristics. These writers thought it was appropriate to make the form, content, and diction of their poetry reflect the highly intellectual atmosphere of the age and the orderly formulaic processes of natural laws.

For the form of his poetry, Pope adopted the closed couplet[4], sometimes called **heroic couplet** in English verse. The **closed couplet** consists of two lines of rhymed iambic pentameter, having a slight pause after the first line, and a heavy pause, or stop, after the second line. Take, for example, the first two lines of Pope's "Essay on Criticism."

> 'Tis hard to say if greater Want of Skill
> Appear in writing or in judging ill;

If we scan these lines, we see that there are five iambs[5] per line. (Five iambs per line constitute **iambic pentameter**.)

[3] diction: the choice and use of words, phrases, sentence structure, etc. in speaking or writing
[4] couplet: two consecutive lines of verse, usually having the same rhyme and meter
[5] iamb: an unstressed syllable followed by a stressed syllable

Notice, also, the rhyming of *Skill* and *ill*, and the long pause after *ill*. In Pope's frame of reference, such precision reflected the precision of mathematics, which was regarded as the ultimate definition of the controlled universe of the eighteenth century. My point is, then, that rhyme and meter are artificial and contrived. They have been imposed on poetry by men who wanted to corral language to conform to conventions, which were made popular by the pressures of society.

In addition to a strict rigid form, Pope and his generation had very particular notions regarding proper subject matter for poetry. Poetry's content had to reflect the highly intellectual achievements of the Enlightenment. Furthermore, since it was thought that society was improving and utopia was approachable, then poetry had to contribute to this development. Therefore, only certain subjects were allowable for good poetry, such as religion, philosophy, moral instruction; or uplifting subjects such as love, natural beauty, and other traditionally inspirational topics. Even an expanded list of the few examples I have provided here would still be highly restrictive and binding. It was merely a sign of the times; these were superimposed rules that had only narrow application to the real substance of poetry.

It was in their choice of words, however, that Pope and his followers went to the utmost extreme. Pope considered the language of poetry to be special and exalted above other usages of language-even the most formally written essays. For Pope, poetic language had to be elevated. For example, the cat never ran around the house; rather, he would be inclined to write that the feline circumambulated the royal edifice with great celerity. Pope's diction was so contrived that only people who care to study his poetry ever obtain any understanding of it today. Inevitably, poets began to question the value of writing poems that could be understood and appreciated by only a small segment of society. They concluded, appropriately, that stilted, contrived language was not essential to good poetry. As the Age of Enlightenment came to a close, a change in the conventions for poetry in that era was on the horizon.

b. What was the goal of the Greeks? How was this reflected in their poetry?

c. How did the Enlightenment change the form and content of poetry?

d. Who was the leading poet of the Enlightenment?

e. What were the particular notions of Pope and his followers regarding the rules of poetry?

f. For this poetry section, you will be referring to *The Mentor Book of Major British Poets* edited by Oscar Williams, published by Penguin Group, ISBN 0-451-6237-0. Briefly look through the book and acquaint yourself with some of the poetry and its poets.

2. a. Poetry as an Agent of Change

Such change corresponded with great political and social changes in Western civilization. By the late 1700's, the world, and especially England, witnessed and experienced the American and French Revolutions. Fortunately for England, God used John Wesley and his contemporaries to create a spiritual resistance to anarchy, and political change came without revolutionary war. Much of the pressure for social change in England derived from the dark side of the Industrial Revolution. As England slowly went from an agrarian to an industrial society, the people seemed abandon their traditional values. As their traditional agrarian society changed, and masses of people were forced to leave their small familyplots and work in the overcrowded, oppressive industrial districts. By 1800, the leading writers of the age, including William Wordsworth, Samuel Coleridge, William Blake, and John Keats, among others, had taken up the banner for social change, and were writing poems intended to stir the social consciences of the upper class. In this regard, they felt that changes were needed in the form and content of poetry.

Wordsworth and Coleridge published a booklet of poems in 1798 entitled *Lyrical Ballads*. The booklet was reissued in 1800 and 1802 with an expanded "Preface" in which

Wordsworth explained the changes he and Coleridge had made in the poems of *Lyrical Ballads*. First, they decided that rhyme is not essential to poetry, which implies that they would not use the closed couplet exclusively. This frees the poet to choose words to express his true meaning rather than be bound to choosing words to fit a rhyme scheme. In their desire to express themselves more accurately, Wordsworth and Coleridge also repudiated Pope's stilted word usage in favor of words more commonly used in everyday conversation. (It must be remembered, however, that these poets' everyday words were still far more eloquent than what you and I would consider normal conversation.) Additionally, the "Preface" stated that subject matter for poetry must be expanded to include a broad range of personal feelings. Also, the poet should be free to write about social problems and the need to improve. Thus, by the early 1800's, poetry had made considerable changes in form, diction, and subject matter.

By 1914, traditional ways were challenged from every direction. By this time, Karl Marx and Frederick Engels had written convincing arguments against prevailing Western political and economic institutions. Charles Darwin's works, which included *The Descent of Man* (1871), were well accepted by 1914. For those people whose faith was founded only on their social upbringing, and not on a personal born-again relationship with Christ, Darwin's theories seemed reasonable, and their existing faith was shattered. Sigmund Freud's findings showed that the mind could not be perfected through reason, and Albert Einstein proved that there were variables in Newton's orderly mechanical universe. The effects of all these things, in addition to changing social demographics, forced people to reexamine traditional ways and values.

The artist no longer felt that traditional ways in his field could accommodate the changing world of the early 1900's. Up until the latter part of the nineteenth century, Europeans generally felt that life was getting better and there were better times ahead. As approached, however, this optimism had changed to uncertainty and even pessimism. The outbreak of World War I was the breaking point. Not only was the artist horrified, but the whole world was shaken. Even the least involved citizens were pulled, one way or another, into the conflict. Even the least informed person now could see for himself that humanity had not only the capability, but the will to destroy itself. It was equally obvious that traditional means of warfare would not win the war, and this had to change. Thus, the soldier in the trench, the wife and parents at home, all gave up, to some degree, their beliefs in traditional ways of doing things. For the artist, this meant abandoning traditional form, subject matter, and medium.

For the poet, abandoning form meant freeing oneself from rhyme, meter, and difficult patterns, such as the sonnet[6] or villanelle[7]. This, actually, was a good thing. As Milton said in his introduction to *Paradise Lost*, rhyme restricts the poet to find words that fit the scheme leaving his thoughts poorly expressed. Furthermore, rhyme is a man-made convention, and not essential to poetry. The combined effects of rhyme and meter give poetry a song-like effect, which detracts from its meaning. Worse yet, rhyme and meter desensitize one to the natural, God-given sounds and rhythms of language. Without the trappings of rhyme and meter, the poet felt free to choose words to express his meaning exactly. Thus, he granted himself a much enlarged vocabulary. Additionally, common conversational diction was embraced as suitable for poetry. This opened the door for a wide range of possibilities, including dialect[8], stream-of-consciousness[9], and even street language. Without having to choose words conforming to a metrical pattern, the poet was free to exploit the natural rhythms of language.

None of this seemed too appropriate until World War I opened the world's eyes to the destructive power that we could unleash on ourselves. This called for greatly expanding poetic subject matter to accommodate such revelations. Thus, the poet felt free to write about previously unwelcome subjects such as ghastly, horrific, senseless evil, and the effects of such things on one's emotions and outlook on life. Such subjects could not be expressed in flowery language that sounded like a happy song. New expressions were needed, and free verse[10] became the avenue for them to be expressed.

[6] sonnet: a poem consisting of fourteen lines, usually written in iambic pentameter

[7] villanelle: poetry consisting of nineteen lines, divided into six stanzas that includes five tercets and a concluding quatrain (a four-line stanza)

[8] dialect: type of diction spoken by particular groups of people

[9] stream-of-consciousness: a literary technique used to reveal a character's perceptions and thoughts

[10] free verse: poetry consisting of no established pattern of rhyme, meter, and form

b. During the beginning of the 1900's, traditional values were being questioned. Choose at least one of the following individuals, and describe his impact on traditional values: Charles Darwin, Sigmund Freud, Karl Marx, Frederick Engels.

To answer this question, you need a good history book in addition to an encyclopedia. These men made their marks at the right time. To determine their impact, first look at the time in which they lived. What events, such as war, economic collapse, political change, etc., helped shape what people thought? What were the philosophical and religious sentiments of the day? What social conditions prevailed?

3. a. Have We Abandoned Order?

I heard an argument that to abandon rhyme and meter is to abandon a sense of order. Perhaps people who uphold this point of view never had to diagram sentences. For those of us who had to learn the details of grammar and sentence structure, one thing becomes abundantly clear: language has order. Today's poets seem to think that God's given order for language is orderly enough and need not be tampered with.

On the other hand, there are some who would say that rhyme and meter should be thrown out altogether. This, too, is extreme. Rhyme and meter have their place in poetry, and this place is not a thing of the past. What has happened is to adjust the importance of rhyme and meter from their dominant place to their appropriate place as tools which the poet may or may not choose to use. Ten years ago, rhyme and meter were still considerably out of favor. They are making a comeback, however. Today, poems that are well written in strict form are at a high premium. The trick is to write the poem in such a way that the rhyme, meter, and other aspects of form are barely noticeable. The difficulty of writing a good poem in a strict form makes successful attempts special, which is being recognized by those who understand good poetry. Finally, all good poets know the details of rhyme, meter, and strict form. This enables them to avoid the pitfalls while simultaneously using the strengths. The balance seems to be that a good poet should know the traditional conventions of poetry and be able to use such conventions to enrich the content of what he has written rather than to detract from it.

b. As reflected in the poetry of Wordsworth and Coleridge, what changes took place in the form and content of poetry around 1800?

c. What effect did the approach and arrival of World War I have on the poetry of that time?

d. What details should be important to all good poets?

4-5. Find pages vii-viii in *The Mentor Book of Major British Poets.* From the list of poets from William Blake to John Keats, choose one and write two to three paragraphs describing the poet's era, style, and beliefs. Include examples from the poet's work to substantiate your statements. State your reaction to the poet's work as well.

1.

b. The Greeks thought the world was naturally chaotic and sought to bring it into order.

   Their poetry was metrical and had a specific number of syllables per line.

c. Poets of the Enlightenment felt that the form of poetry should reflect the mathematical order of their known universe. Therefore, their poems had a regular meter, strict rhyme scheme, and a specific number of syllables (usually 12) per line. They felt that content should reflect the highest intellectual standards.

d. Alexander Pope was the leading poet of the Enlightenment.

e. Appropriate form was the heroic (or closed) couplet (two lines of rhyming iambic pentameter). Subject matter was to be intellectual and without reference to common, everyday topics. Diction was flowery, exalted, and intellectual.

3.

b. First, rhyme is not essential to poetry. Secondly, diction should not be flowery and ornate, but more along the lines of words used in conversation. Finally, subject matter should be expanded to include items from everyday living.

c. After World War I, political, scientific, and social changes had shaken the foundations of two centuries of traditions. Poets no longer felt that traditional forms and rules for content and diction were appropriate for the Modern Age.

d. Knowing the details of rhyme, meter, and strict form enables the poet to avoid their pitfalls while simultaneously using their strengths.

1. a. Language is Poetic

Although **free verse** is the prevailing choice among today's poets, there is no reason to think that we are fellowshipping a rebellious spirit if we write in this manner. Free verse does not mean sloppy, uncontrolled, or deliberately offensive. It merely means free from conventions. Since one of the chief aims of poetry is to say a great deal in a limited space, many poets feel that free verse enables them to condense their thoughts into the tightest, most meaningful language.

The beauty of language and the possibilities of language are not lost in free verse. In fact, free verse sometimes helps us to appreciate language and to exploit its natural sounds and rhythms to the fullest. Take, for example, the title of this chapter:

Lan guage is Po e tic

First, there is a natural contrast between the slow, soft sounds of "Language is," and the quick, staccato sounds of "Poetic." We start slowly, but finish sharply. The soft consonant sounds of "Language is" make us drawl, and the sharp consonants of "Poetic" make us accelerate over the word as if the slow start has made us eager to make up for lost time. The accent on the first syllable seems to emphasize its ponderous sound, whereas the accent on the fifth syllable seems to emphasize the abrupt ending. Poets have learned to be sensitive to these natural sounds and rhythms. Since words are the building blocks of poetry, every word is a resource which may be examined for its potential usefulness in the context of sound, rhythm, and above all, meaning.

The primary goal of the poet should be to express the precise meaning of his thoughts. To do this, we choose words which convey our meaning, and eliminate words which do not. Thus, we must learn to recognize abstractions, and eliminate them from the language of poetry.

Anyone who has taken a creative writing course, especially

for poetry, has heard the terms **abstract** and **concrete**. It was taught that abstractions are to be avoided and everything must be concrete. Words that are concrete can be grasped by one or more of the five senses. Abstract words cannot be grasped. Abstractions are undefinable, and therefore contrary to the poet's mission, which is to convey precise meaning. Abstractions can be represented with concrete examples and it is one of the poet's jobs to provide clear language which brings the abstract down to the concrete.

A short list of abstractions that are commonly used by inexperienced poets generally includes such words as *love*, *beauty*, *truth*, *heart*, *honesty*, etc. The great philosophers, the great Bible scholars, and even the Bible itself have not defined these words. St. Paul gave examples of what love is and is not, but did not attempt to define it. Consider the phrase "I love you." We generally take this to mean romantic love, but the possibilities for this phrase are endless. These words can be applied between a parent and child. However, the love between parent and child ranges from inseparable bonding to stern discipline, and all emotional stops in between. A young man might pick up a baseball and say "I love you" with all conviction. He might be referring to the pleasure he derives as a player, or just to a general delight as a spectator. If the ball has been signed by his favorite player, he might be referring to the uniqueness of this trophy or to its potential dollar value, or the memory of the incidence of its signing. Thus, the abstraction, *love*, must have a specific example that must be conveyed in words which are apprehendable with the senses. Allow me to expound the list of abstractions, and wait to explain more about making a poem concrete. In addition to words already mentioned, some of the most common abstractions are *sincerity*, *warmth*, *happiness*, *joy*, *sadness*, *evil*, *holy*, *peace*, *grief*, *wholeness*, *oneness*, *ideal*, *glory*...you get the idea.

b. Write definitions for the words *abstract* and *concrete* in relation to poetry. Give at least two examples of each.

Note: A common extension of an abstract word is an abstract phrase, sentence, or even an entire poem in the abstract. Often, my students seemed to confuse abstraction with the power of suggestion. They would argue that they wanted the poem to be full of generalizations so that the reader would take them and make them specific in his own interpretation. This always resulted in failure, because such poems were so general in nature that no one understood them, or perhaps the poem was understood, but no one found it interesting. The power of suggestion is in the concrete, not the abstract. You are unlikely to establish a rapport with your reader unless you provide him with specific details in which he can easily identify with you.

c. Read some poetry from *The Mentor Book of Major British Poets*. Try reading some poetry aloud.

2. a. The Most Important Job: Choosing Your Subject

Whenever we talk about our choice of words, we are also talking about content. Today, content outweighs all other considerations for poetry. Therefore, choosing words which precisely express our meaning is a top priority. The first step in obtaining content is to choose a subject.

The pressure to free the writer to write about subjects of his choice reached the breaking point after World War I. Today, we are free to write about any subject we choose. This has led to conflicts for many people, especially Christians. A good many of the best poets presently writing are highly critical of society and the individuals who comprise it. They rarely see anything good about social institutions, value systems, or life itself, whether that life is theirs or someone else's. Recognizing this, many Christians feel duty bound to fight these perspectives by writing demonstrably preachy poems with the goal of glorifying the Lord. Unfortunately, not one such poem which ever appeared in any of my workshops was a good poem. Most were not even salvageable. Thus, the goal was not reached, because a poor poem, regardless of its intent, seldom glorifies the Lord.

As far as suitable subject matter for Christian poets, you have the same freedom as anyone else. Remember, however, that worshipful or preachy poems are likely to be dismissed as unoriginal and dull. If you have truly become

[11] stanza: the grouping of lines in poetry, set off by a space, usually having a pattern of rhyme and meter

a Christian, and your mind is renewed, then your perspective on your life's experience will reflect that. A Christian outlook glorifies God without having to say so. Your poems will glorify Christ by showing His perspective on your life's experiences–should those experiences be uplifting or not. I might add that it can be edifying to write about those experiences which are not uplifting, as some of the Psalms clearly demonstrate. However, we can't dwell on the undesirable so much that we convey pessimism, hopelessness, self-pity, etc.

A well-crafted poem glorifies the Lord. Craft involves everything from well chosen words to correct punctuation. A poorly crafted poem is easy to detect, and will be held in low esteem, regardless of the content or the high enthusiasm of the poet. Therefore, to glorify God, strive to be a master of the craft, and show a Christ-like perspective on things. Finally, if "the earth is the Lord's and the fullness thereof," then use the fullness of subject matter available to you.

b. Look at five or more Psalms. Identify the emotion being conveyed in each. Are there any concrete descriptions used?

c. Stop and Review
   1) Language has natural sounds and rhythms.
   2) Language used in poetry can be abstract or concrete.
   3) The more concrete the description, the clearer the meaning of the poem.
   4) The content of a poem is of greatest importance.

3. a. Form
Once you have selected a subject to write about, you might want to consider what form your poem should be in. What I mean by form is any prescribed pattern for rhyme, meter, line length, or stanza[11]. A form might be simple, such as following a rhyme scheme like the couplet. Forms might involve more than rhyme scheme, such as the **Shakespearean sonnet**, in which the first four lines (quatrain) develop a theme, the next two quatrains consist of variations on the theme, and the last two lines summarize the quatrains, sort of pulling them all together. This is a

tough assignment, and rarely achieved with excellence by even the best of poets.

Today, the poet is free to choose a traditional form, to choose free verse and disregard form, or to make up a form of his own. I suggest that beginners use free verse, due to the difficulty of writing in strict forms. This allows you to concentrate on the substance of poetry and not be distracted by difficult procedural restrictions.

Once you have chosen an overall form, then the poem may or may not be broken down into stanzas. Many of today's poems have no stanzas. A **stanza** is like a poetic paragraph, and traditionally consists of a number of lines in a regular form, which, once established, is repeated over the length of the poem. Stanzas are still in use but tend to be irregular in form. Today's stanzas are sometimes only recognizable when we see the stanza break. The stanza break occurs when a line is left blank, usually, but not always, between the end of one sentence and the beginning of another. Stanza breaks are useful when the poet is switching directions, or introducing a new thought. Stanza breaks tell the reader that there is a break in transition from one thought to another, and are helpful in avoiding confusion.

b. Write a definition for the term stanza.

c. After stanzas, the next significant unit of poetry is the **line**. Today, line length can be any length you want. However, experiments with line length are generally considered outdated, and most poems have rather modest line length, averaging between six and twelve to fourteen syllables. Once line length is established, it tends to remain fairly consistent throughout.

A few guidelines that seem to be general principles might help you determine your lines. Most of today's poets do not like to pause after every line. A line without punctuation at the end is called a run-on, and today's poets use **run-on** lines or **enjambment** liberally to avoid tedious predictability. Many poets begin a line with an insignificant word, such as an article or preposition, but end a line with a word of substance. This, too, can become a pattern, however, and once a pattern is established the poet will break it to avoid dull repetition.

Another general consideration is rather vague, and depends much more on intuition than any clear guidelines. One might say that line length depends on what portion of the poem the poet wants you to see at a given glance. In the minds of many poets, there is the idea that a line of poetry might stand in isolation. The poet wants you to chew on his work a line at a time, and each line becomes a sort of unit with boundaries controlled by the writer. Thus, the poem consists of significant units, which build one after the other, until the final construction is complete. I can only say that experience will enable you to grasp this concept and you will develop a sense of line length as you develop your individual style.

d. The following poem might serve to illustrate some of the points made so far:

Hideyoshi's Castle

1 Although things have changed
since the old warlord conquered
feudal kingdoms around him,
Hideyoshi would be proud
5 that his castle still rises
in a pyramid
of seven orderly tiers,
the upturned eaves like wooden scrolls.

From its top, you see idlers
10 sunk in the park lawn, tourists
strolling among flowering trees,
fat goldfish in the moat
around a quarry wall
that rises like a stone fortress,
15 between the castle
and encroaching Osaka

where streamlined monoliths
dominate the sky. Pavement, ordering
the land, advances relentlessly

20 toward distant factories
that shape materials
for TVs, cameras, cars,
stamped Germany, France, U.S.A.
These economic regiments
25 march off assembly lines in ranks,
seize world markets,
occupy foreign businesses, homes.

Occasionally, a worker
stops, straightens his back,
30 looks past the abandoned airstrip,
beyond the deserted WW II barracks,
and smiles, revived
at the sight of Hideyoshi's castle.

e. The subject of the poem is Hideyoshi's castle, which has been preserved and made into a public park. Hideyoshi was the first of Japan's feudal warlords to bring the other feudal kingdoms under his control, unifying all of Japan for the first time.

The poem consists of thirty-three lines, the shortest of which have four syllables (lines 15, 26, 32), and the longest, eleven syllables (line 31). Although some of the lines stand in isolation, some do not. However, there is a progression that gives a little something to chew on in each line. There are four irregular stanzas, with no punctuation between stanzas two and three. Over half the lines (nineteen in all) have no punctuation to pause the reader at the end.

As in every poem, there is a narrator, sometimes called the speaker of the poem. Most often, the narrator is the author himself, but sometimes the author uses other people to narrate his poem. He might choose to have a friend, relative, animal, object, or fictional character narrate the poem. Your choice of narrator is just as open as any other writer of fiction. In "Hideyoshi's Castle," the narrator appears to be a foreigner making observations about Japanese culture and society.

In the first stanza, the narrator describes the castle from a point outside the castle. The next stanza abruptly switches place to the top of the structure, from where the narrator can see the city. There is no description of the journey through the park and up into the interior of the castle. Such a description does not contribute to the poem's content. The stanza break shows us that a distinct change has taken place, and the reader is ready to shift to another plane. Stanza three shows the narrator's reflection on what he sees. He is impressed by the industrial energy of the city and describes this in military images. Stanza four suggests there are reminders of World War II still visible and that the militaristic attitude of the war has been taken by the Japanese corporate empires.

Oftentimes, students in my workshops are bound by representing an experience exactly as it happened. This can be paralyzing, since exactly what happened might not make a very good poem. For example, we do not know if anything the narrator describes from the top of Hideyoshi's castle is actually there. The speaker's observations are entirely conjectural and no evidence is given to substantiate his connection between World War II and the present industrial society. Lastly, it is highly unlikely that the Japanese have allowed the reminders of World War II to remain. It is likely that military installations have been converted to productive use. Therefore, the poet created a few imaginary lines to support a position he wants to take. This is quite fair and even desirable, because poems are works of the imagination, and you may use any means you have to convey a certain message for your poem.

One final note regarding form. Distortions of form and disregard for sentence structure, punctuation, and mechanics are considered outdated and immature. The experiments of e.e. cummings worked well for him, but today's poets have returned to predominantly standard procedures. It is expected that you will have complete sentences, except when variations might emphasize your content. Furthermore, you are expected to use standard punctuation and mechanics, since these are unnoticeable. As a result, the reader will concentrate on your words, and not be distracted by mechanical gimmickry. If you want to deviate from standard measures, do so sparingly. It takes skill to deviate from the standard and make it work for you. I suggest beginners stay on safe ground.

f. Define the following terms. (You may refer to the *Literary Terms* found in the back of this book.) Locate examples of each using *The Mentor Book of Major British Poets* or another poetry book of your choice.

1) couplet
2) quatrain
3) Shakespearean sonnet
4) villanelle
5) free verse

4-5. Find pages viii - x in *The Mentor Book of Major British Poets.* From the list of poets from Tennyson to Hardy, choose one and write two to three paragraphs describing the poet's era, style, and beliefs. Include examples from the poet's work to substantiate your statements. State your reaction to the poet's work as well.

1.

b. Abstract: having no specific meaning and no objective association. Abstractions cannot be defined and must have examples to help illustrate the point.
Examples: love, beauty, truth, goodness, spirit

Concrete: something real, specific, and able to be grasped and understood through the five senses.
Examples: rock, wood, steak, dog, orange

3.

b. Stanza: Traditionally, a stanza is a grouping within a poem consisting of a set number of lines written in a pattern, usually having a regular rhyme and meter. The stanza, once established, is repeated throughout the poem.

Today's stanzas are usually irregular, without a repeating pattern. They are sometimes distinguishable only by the stanza break, which is a blank line indicating a change in thought, scene, etc.

f.

1) couplet - two consecutive lines of poetry, usually having the same rhyme and meter
2) quatrain - a four-line stanza with a rhyme scheme abbaabba; and a sestet usually with rhyme scheme cdcdcd or cdecde
3) Shakespearean sonnet - three quatrains and a couplet, usually with a rhyme scheme of abab cdcd efef gg
4) villanelle - poetry consisting of nineteen lines, divided into six stanzas that includes five tercets and a concluding quatrain
5) free verse - poetry without a particular pattern of rhyme, meter, or stanza

1. a. Getting Ready to Write

Word Usage

**Diction** is one's choice of words. One of the poet's top priorities is to choose the most effective words to convey his message. Having already mentioned the importance of the concrete as opposed to the abstract, we can proceed with other considerations involving diction. Here are a few present day guidelines.

Today's poets try to use language that comes close to what is found in conversation. The common guideline for many poets is to obtain a conversational tone to the poem. Obviously, there are limitations as to how conversational we can be. For example, it is not conversational to speak in complete, fluid sentences, yet your poem should be written that way. Also, we use abstractions in our conversation, but they are deadly to poetry. Clichés[12], likewise, are useful in conversation, but highly undesirable for poetry. The trick to a conversational tone is to use words that are normally contained in our speaking vocabulary, with some exceptions to refine our meaning when necessary. It is unnecessary is to go out of the way to be flowery and intellectual; to play word games; to be overly sound conscious, as with rhyme and meter. Just write down your thoughts with the words that come to your mind, and worry about refining your diction after your thoughts are fully expressed.

Since many of the greatest poems ever written were composed anywhere from one to four hundred years ago and beyond, it is understandable that the diction of such poems will influence our concepts of proper poetic language. One such influence includes **archaisms**. These are word constructions which are no longer in use. Some common examples are *o'er* for *over*, *e'er* for *ever*, *thou*, *wouldst*, *couldst*, etc. In short, you don't want your poetry to sound like the King James Bible. Closely associated with archaisms are interjections, the most common of which is *Oh!* Others include *Ah!*, *Ho!*, *Yeah!* and are commonly used to indicate one's emotional overflow. The present day position on this is that your poem should inspire such

[12]cliché: an expression that has become trite from overuse

emotions without your telling us to have them. The content inspires the emotion, not an interjection with an exclamation point. Another form of obsolete language usage is the syntactical inversion. **Syntax,** the order of words in a sentence, is expected to be normal, except when skillful rearrangement produces emphasis or a nuance of meaning. However, such inversions as *would I* for *I would, Often do I* for *I often do*, *then should I* for *I should then*, etc., are no longer acceptable. Readers of the King James translation of the Bible are going to have to be especially alert not to use such syntax.

I have already mentioned that sound and rhythm are still sought after in poetry, although they are secondary to meaning. We are fortunate in that the natural sounds and rhythms of language are sufficient to produce satisfying linguistic pleasure. However, one more thing to consider in this light is the sense of sound to emphasize meaning. Take, for example, the words "Giant hot fudge sundae." We not only picture the sundae and almost feel its weight, but the words themselves have a heavy, ponderous sound to them. If we picture a person who is equally heavy and ponderous, the words emphasize the image even more. The same can be said for "Gentle muscle massage." The sound of this phrase is soft, smooth, relaxing, highlighting the meaning. This is not **onomatopoeia**, in which the word or near word deliberately imitates a sound, such as *meow*, *moo*, etc. Onomatopoeia is overt, whereas finding a connection between sound and meaning is subtle, and is much more appreciated by today's poets.

b. Think of three objects that are distinctive in use or appearance. Write a three-word description of each object using language in which the sound emphasizes its meaning.

2. a. Image

If you have attended a creative writing course or read a book on creative writing, you have undoubtedly been admonished to "Show us, don't tell us." Applied to poetry, this means that we are to have the narrator approximate what a movie camera does. That is, provide the visual and audio, the action, dialogue, and everything necessary to round out the picture. Once the picture is complete, the poet need not explain what is meant. The message should be evident in the poem without explanation.

The favorite device for poets to convey their messages is through the use of the **image**. Although the image is primarily a word picture, it is much more than description of the visual. An image may involve all of the five senses. If you want to involve your reader, let him see, taste, smell, touch, and hear your images.

b. Consider the following poem:

Takahashi's House

1 The frame of Takahashi's house
is made of posts and beams
joined without nails.
A faint odor clings
5 to ancient dark wood.
We wore sweaters in the heatless room
and lolled on the straw mat floor
watching baseball in color.
I looked outside and saw
10 two women in a rice paddy
wearing cone-shaped hats,
stooped at the waist,
moving their arms like
slow train wheels.
15 A sharp grounder to short.
"Double play!"
shouted Takahashi's son,
while his mother sat
cross-legged in her kimono,
20 admiring the silk tapestry.

c. The narrator, a foreigner and probably an American, relates to us his impressions from inside the house of a Japanese family. The poem consists of a series of images, mostly visual, but not entirely. For example, the first five lines give us a glimpse of the house's interior. Line 4 adds an "odor" to the visual description, emphasizing the age of the wood. In line 6, the words *sweaters* and *heatless* are tactile, and the shouted "Double play!" gives us something to hear. The poem is about the contrast between the old and the new, as well as the East and the West. However, we are not told this. The contrasting images show us, instead. The first seven lines describe the old house, which has no central heat and no chairs. By contrast, line 8 shows us two modern items, both of which have been introduced from the West. Furthermore, since television requires electricity, we realize that heating the house would be no problem should Takahashi choose to do so.

Next, we are back in old Japan, watching the women harvest rice in the way of long, long ago. Takahashi's son apparently knows a few words of English, and is fairly well informed about baseball, bringing us back to the present and the influence of the West. Have you noticed, yet, how dull my explanation of the poem is? I certainly hope so, because this dull explanation shows the difference between telling and showing. The images are far more interesting than the explanation, wouldn't you agree? This is a common way to develop a poem.

d. Choose several poems. Search for images that appeal to each of the senses: visual, auditory, tactile, olfactory, and taste. Locate at least one image for each sense.

3. a. Symbols

Images are not difficult, and can be managed by any aspiring poet. Symbols, on the other hand, seem to be extremely difficult. A **symbol** is something which represents something else. A symbol is objective and can have numerous associations. Perhaps the most complex symbol is the cross. The cross represents the death of Christ, all that His death signifies, and therefore represents Christianity itself. The things we associate with the cross are numerous and complex, and the power of this symbol is enormous for believers and nonbelievers alike.

For some reason, inexperienced poets are quite fond of symbols. Unfortunately, these symbols are often all alike, and therefore ridiculously cliché. Some of the most common symbols include rivers, mountains, and deserts. These natural barriers are used as symbols of obstacles in life to overcome. The narrator of the poem always heroically overcomes these obstacles, usually suffering terribly in the process, shedding numerous tears along the way. Seeds are also popular, since they represent something small which can grow into something huge, like a tree. Silver and gold seeds planted in among humans develop good characteristics, whereas black or disfigured seeds spread evil. Animals are common symbols which seem always to have the same interpretation, depending on the characteristics of the animal. For some of you, I know I have accurately described what you have written. I know that you have invested considerable emotion and strong privately held feelings in your poem. Be advised, however, that symbols rarely work, especially for beginning poets.

b. Metaphor, Simile, and Personification

How, then, can we obtain depth to our poetry without the use of symbols? The easy answer is to use metaphors. A **metaphor** is a comparison between two things not usually considered to have much in common. If the comparison is implied or suggested, we use the term metaphor. If the comparison is direct, using the words *like* or *as*, it is called a **simile**. These are not difficult to create and are highly useful in making poetry more interesting.

c. Consider the following poem:

Castle Grounds at Hirosaki

1 The four-story guardhouse
is all that remains
of the castle at Hirosaki.
Its wooden floor creaks wearily
5 as I walk toward the stairs.
A mild stable odor comes
from hanging saddles stained
by sweaty men and horses.
Samurai armor is nailed to walls.
10 I ascend, where
steel swords, crossed

like folded hands, reflect
the keen edge of desperate combat.
As I pass
15 under their hostile points,
the fragrance of cherry blossoms
clears my head before I reach
the open window and look down.
The trees are white anemones,
20 tentacles swaying.
In patches among them, colors flip
as reclining people move
to eat fish, rice, and sip drinks.
Globular notes rise
25 like escaped balloons
from a mixture of song
and conversation.
Beyond the white-trimmed moat,
green foothills slither away,
30 bunch against mountains
where winter snow still clings.

d. Once again, the narrator observes something and reports his observations. The observations are not as subjective in this poem and the narrator might be any nationality. Like Hideyoshi's castle, the grounds at Hirosaki have been turned into a park. The narrator tells us that the castle is gone and we infer that the guardhouse has been made into a museum. The first metaphor appears in line 4. The "wooden floor" is said to "creak wearily." Weariness is only characteristic of animate objects, not inanimate ones. This kind of metaphor is called a **personification**, in which a characteristic attributable to people has been given to an inanimate object or animal. The metaphor suggests that the floor is infirm, like a person who has become weary. In this context, we infer that the floor is probably old and weak, as well.

Lines 11 and 12 comprise a simile. The folded hands suggest that the swords are now harmlessly at rest. Line 15 is another personification, attributing hostility to the swords, as if they have an attitude to repel, despite being hung over the lintel. Lines 19 and 20 compare the cherry trees to sea anemones. This shows us that the trees are in full bloom and that the narrator is high above them. You get the idea.

Other metaphors in this poem describe musical notes like balloons, foothills that slither, and the narrator's head is cleared. Note that none of these metaphors are particularly difficult. You might be able to do as well or better given the same experience to describe. My point is that the use of metaphors is a great way to enrich the content of poetry, and metaphors are relatively easy to handle and often succeed.

e. Define the following terms. Locate examples of these terms in poetry, or make up your own: image, metaphor, simile, personification.

Note: It is a good idea to find definitions for these terms in other sources, such as a textbook or dictionary, in order to enlarge your understanding.

4. a. How to Develop a Poem

Sometimes when we have an idea, it is difficult to put into words. Many poets simply write out their thoughts without regard to making them poetic. They just want to get the thoughts down so that nothing is forgotten. I recommend this practice. For some reason, many beginning writers want to put their thoughts in finished form in the first writing. They bog down, trying to write a polished work as many ideas are surfacing. This causes the writer to have to suppress the ideas that are forming in favor of concentrating on achieving perfection. Thus, the stage of inspiration that produces the ideas is pushed aside and the thoughts are lost. Therefore, when you are in a reflective mood, just relax, jot down your thoughts, and don't suppress the early brainstorming process. This brainstorming process is a natural thought pattern which is sometimes very special and should be encouraged. You can worry about finishing your poem later.

Looking again at "Castle Grounds at Hirosaki," we see one of the most common ways of developing a poem. The poem is a **dramatization**, in which the narrator simply shares an experience by starting at place *A* and walking us to place *B*, *C*, etc. The narrator acts as a movie camera, recording his observations as he goes, and reporting the sequence of events to us. There is no attempt to add commentary about what is observed. The speaker of the poem is satisfied to let the sequence of images show us the meaning of the poem.

Basically, "Castle Grounds at Hirosaki" records one short event. The narrator walks from the first floor of the watchtower of a feudal castle, reaches the top, and looks down through an open window. The poem divides in half between the ascension of the stairs and the observations from the window. While inside the guardhouse, the narrator sees images of Japan's feudal warlike past, which make him feel uneasy and threatened. However, the images from the window describe an entirely different Japan, as the narrator shares his sense of appreciation for the peaceful, harmonious society of the present. The fact that the guardhouse and castle grounds have been made into a public park serves to emphasize the contrast between the old and new Japan.

b. The following poem is developed much the same way as "Castle Grounds at Hirosaki":

John and Mary at Misawa AFB

1 John stops at the NCO club
after work to visit with the boys.
He drives home in his Chevy, past
the rows of white, light green,
5 and pale yellow houses, made
of concrete block, lawns mowed
to specification, hedges
of boxwood or redtip. Pot roast
and potatoes are on the table
10 as he arrives. Mary can't wait
to tell him what happened
at bridge club, and the Martin's
boy is seeing some Japanese girl.
Well, tonight is bowling league,
15 so they leave instructions
for the baby-sitter to put
Billy and Sally to bed right
after *Little House on the Prairie.*
In the morning, John watches

20 the kids leave for the bus,
cute with cowboy boots
and Roy Rogers lunch pails.
Sipping coffee, he tells Mary
not to bother with breakfast,
25 those doughnuts at the shop
will do just fine.

c. This poem is also a dramatization. Although the time lapsed in this poem is about sixteen hours, whereas "Castle Grounds at Hirosaki" records about five minutes, there is no difference in dramatic technique except one. The narrator is not in the poem itself. Instead, the narrator records the movements of another person whom he calls John. Rather than the narrator serving as the movie camera itself, we might say that he holds the camera on John, Mary, and family. This, too, is a common way to develop a poem. The writer creates a character and then creates a dramatic sequence for it. I say *it*, because a character can be an animal or a personified object-we're not limited strictly to people, especially in poetry.

As for "John and Mary at Misawa AFB," the speaker of the poem has made an observation. American servicemen stationed in Japan often have very little appreciation for and interaction with Japanese society and culture. The narrator does not want to implicate himself, so he chooses someone else, in this case John, to represent the American position. Having chosen a character, the narrator simply selects a few typical American images which can be selected from myriads available to him as he looks around the base. Then, he puts John through his paces, showing us that John and his family created an American life on Japanese soil, and that all their friends did the same thing. Many of today's poets like this technique. Some poets create characters which surface again and again, providing a different glimpse of our world each time. We say such poems are written in the third person, whereas "Castle Grounds at Hirosaki" is written in the first person.

So far, the poems used as examples in these lessons have not editorialized. That is to say, the narrator has made no **commentary** on what he observes. He merely shares an experience with us, and then leaves it to the reader to decide what meaning there is to be revealed. Often, however, poets make commentary on their poems. Sometimes they wait until the end of the poem, or they make commentary as they go. This can be risky, because commentary must not tell us what the poem means by summarizing what has been written. Commentary must add to what precedes it. In this way, the poet shares with us a revelation which his experience has given him.

d. The following poem is full of commentary:

A Father's Prayer

1 Seated near the incubator, I watched
the nurse handle my son, Nathan Gregory,
7 lbs., 12 oz. Pierced with a long needle,
he winced, and was given to me in a blanket,
5 crying. Son, the shot is for immunization,
the pain necessary. At karate school,
Takahashi did thousands of kicks
and punches every morning, then trained
all afternoon, just to gain a moment's speed.
10 My dad raised me like a potato.
Now I have lumps all over me,
shoots everywhere, with plenty
of people ready to cut them off. Some even
try to cut me up for stew, mash me, fry me.
15 What else are potatoes good for?
I'll train you from the start, as Takahashi
did with his son. You might not teach English
like me, but I'll prune the lumps and shoots
from whatever shape you take.

20 Takahashi knew the value of teaching
his children, and often took his son
out back of the house to see the family
graveyard. The Bible also says tutor
your children, and I have examples
25 of my own to make the lessons clear,
in hope, someday, you'll understand
this father's prayer:

Nathan, bury yourself next to me with
the family. Tell your children to visit,
30 remember our instructions, follow our ways,
that while they live we'll be with them,
and in death we might see them again.

e. The event of the son's birth triggers a series of reflections and personal insights from the father. The first of these begins in line 6, as the father relates the necessary pain from the injection to the necessary pain from hard training, both of which produce good results. The father, however, digresses further in the second stanza, revealing his personal reflection about his own upbringing. Lines 16-19 show an even further dimension to this thought process. The father has learned from his experience that careful attention to raising a child is desirable for the child, which is something that he apparently admired about Takahashi's relationship with his son. Notice, however, that the father admires the relationship, but not the goal. In closing the stanza, the father observed that Takahashi seemed to have his son's future decided, and this must be rejected in favor of encouraging Nathan to pursue his aptitudes and desires. Thus, stanza two consists of reflections on child rearing and commentary regarding what those reflections mean. It reiterates the father's admiration for Takahashi's attentiveness to his son. However, the father recognizes that he cannot raise Nathan in the Japanese tradition of Takahashi, but must raise him in the Western tradition which he feels is right for Nathan. After all this reflection and commentary, we are brought back to the present, in which the father prays for his son. We conclude that family unity means a great deal to the father, perhaps because his own father seemed so uninterested in his development.

This kind of poetic technique is common. You must be careful, however. If, by sharing an experience, it is already obvious what conclusions you want the reader to make, then don't provide a commentary. Remember, it is better that you have shown us rather than told us. Sometimes a combination of techniques can be used.

f. What is commentary?

g. How should commentary affect a poem?

h. Choose a poem to read that contains commentary. Note: Most commentary comes at the end of a poem. Look for poems that describe a scene or episode, etc., then provide the personal meaning of the experience in the last few lines of the poem.

5. a. Once again, the poet begins by sharing a personal experience.

Blossoms

1 Yoshida tried to explain how
the cherry blossom
is like a kamikaze pilot.
I suppose that each blooms vigorously
5 only to spin crazily to earth,
extinguishing its ephemeral glory.

This much I do understand:
Whenever stars appear, I remember
the white branches overhead
10 and my close-up picture freezing
a sprig of flowers in air.

Five white petals,
the size of bee wings
and as delicate,
15 lightly embrace a pale pink
star-shaped center.

Clusters are
firmly set against
the soft blue sky.

b. Lines 3-6 show the narrator's reflection on this experience. He not only tells us what he thinks Yoshida meant, but tells us what it means to him. The thought of the cherry blossom triggers a memory which is provided in stanza two. Actually, there are two memories. The first involves seeing a tree full of blossoms, and the second involves a picture showing a cluster of blossoms close-up. So far, there are two main metaphors. One, the cherry blossom is like a kamikaze pilot, and two, a cluster of blossoms is like the stars at night. There is imagery throughout the first two stanzas, but stanza three is all imagery, detailing a description of a single blossom. A metaphor compares the individual petals to bee wings.

There is no direct transition between the third and last stanzas. Rather, the last stanza refers back to all the other three. It sort of summarizes the poem, but it is only an image, not an editorial commentary. Thus, the poet uses various techniques, mixing them along the way. "Clusters" certainly refers to clusters of cherry blossoms, but also to clusters of stars, and also suggests clusters of zeroes with kamikaze pilots.

The last two lines provide a good example of sound and meaning. "Firmly set against" has a solid sound to it. The line ends abruptly, suggesting firmness, resolve. The last line, by contrast, has a soft sound to it, emphasizing the contrast between the kamikaze pilots and the delicate cherry blossoms.

The metaphor comparing cherry blossoms and kamikaze pilots gives the poem some depth. Although the blossoms and the pilots die and are gone, the memory of them survives. In stanza two, we also see the picture, which survives, and the stars, which are permanent and unchanging. Thus, the poem contrasts that which is long lasting and permanent with that which is organic and dies. This is a common theme in poetry.

These few suggestions for how to develop a poem will, I hope, give you some direction. I worry, however, that some of you might somehow think that these suggestions are rules. Please don't misunderstand my intentions. There are no rules for developing a poem. These are only suggestions to help you get started, until you develop a method of your own with which you are comfortable.

c. Describe the technique called dramatization. Tell how this device is used in poetry.

3.

e. Image: In poetry, the image is a concrete, objective description usually emphasizing the visual, but also might include the other senses such as audio, taste, touch, and smell.

Metaphor: A comparison between two things not usually thought to be related.

Simile: A metaphor in which the comparison is direct, using the words *like* or *as* in the associations.

Personification: A metaphor in which an object is given characteristics associated with human behavior.

4.

f. Commentary, or editorializing, occurs when the narrator pauses to interpret his experience by making conclusions, observations, insights, or other means of personally evaluating his experience.

g. Such commentary must add to the content of your poem. If you already have shown your reader what you mean, then don't editorialize.

5.

c. A dramatization occurs when a character is placed in a situation and relates what happens from his point of view as the scene unfolds. Note: First person narrative always uses *I*, whereas third person uses *he* or *she.*

1-5.

a. Getting started is a matter of finding some subject about which to write. Generally speaking, the easiest subjects to write about derive from a personal experience which had a strong emotional impact on us. Since emotions are wide ranging, we generally have many experiences to choose from. Even very young poets will have little difficulty.

Your goal as a poet, however, is not merely to convey an emotional experience. As an individual, you have a unique way of seeing things. Your goal is to express your unique thoughts concerning the observations you have made about your experiences. Although you might have had an experience common to nearly everyone, you made observations that are uniquely your own. This is what you are striving to convey.

Once the easy subjects are exhausted, then one has to begin searching. When this process begins, then it is time to make close observations of your daily experiences. The challenge here is to take something ordinary and make it extraordinary. Thus you write something which creates a common response in all your readers, while giving them a special twist that enables them to see the unusual in the ordinary. I once heard of a professor who required his students to write a poem a day. I never required that of my students, but perhaps I should have. Such an assignment demanded of those students that they create a poem from the ordinary daily student grind. If you keep a notebook in which you jot down some observation on a daily basis, you'll be surprised what comes of it. Keeping such a notebook-whether you do so daily, weekly, or whatever -will help you generate ideas for poems.

There were some rather gifted poets in one of the poetry workshops I attended. A particularly good poet, who was already widely known and broadly published, made the suggestion that the workshop take some field trips in order to generate material for more poems. Although he was a prolific writer of excellent poetry, he was sharing his frustration with writer's block. It was good to hear from such an accomplished poet that he could get stuck for subject matter as easily as the rest of us. This writer often takes his suggestion personally and goes on excursions of his own, often with his wife and perhaps a couple friends, and then write something about the day's activities. He sometimes worked the poems about these little jaunts into powerful pieces which were published in the best periodicals. When we depart from the daily routine to enjoy a field trip, vacation, or just an afternoon away from the house, our senses are refreshed and this can be highly stimulating to our creativity. Whenever you take a diversion like this, make it a goal for yourself to write at least one poem about the experience.

Another way of getting started is to choose a subject you have strong feelings about, then select your material to support your topic. For example, you might feel that society is anti-family, and you want to make a statement to the contrary. By now, I hope you know that a poet does not write speeches. You have to select from your experience those things which show us your position. Thus, you might show us what your household activities are when you first get up, or on a busy weekend, or at the basketball courts. The point is, that you have certain things you do that, for you, say "This is family." Those are the sights, sounds, and odors, etc., that will convey your sentiments in poetic fashion.

It can be helpful to make a list of things that you feel strongly about and select material to show how you feel. This can be treacherous, however, because you run the risk of being preachy. Leave the preaching for later if someone asks you why you have such a love for family, children, or whatever. Let your poetry do the preaching, so to speak, through the craft of poetry. Otherwise, you might as well just write an essay and let it go at that.

Let me conclude this by reiterating that it can be helpful to make a list of things that you feel strongly about and write poems for these topics. You will probably get some pretty good poems out of this if you are careful. This is because if you have strong feelings about something, you tend to write strong poetry. You will find that your intensity level will probably be high as you take on your strongest feelings.

b. Keep a journal this week. Daily, write your thoughts, activities, and events of the day.

c. Write a poem using dramatization about an event or experience.

1. a. Continue the journal writing for another week.

   b. Attempt to write a poem about an event or experience using first person.

2. Write a poem about the same event (from **1b**) or another event, but this time, write the poem from the third person.

3-4. Make a list of at least four topics about which you feel strongly. Remembering that concrete images are better than abstract ones, attempt to write a poem about one of your topics.

5. Share your work with a parent, teacher, or friend. Ask him to tell you what the poem communicates to him. Be open to hear his thoughts and suggestions. If his understanding does not match your intention, attempt to revise your poem for greater clarity. Have the poem reviewed again.

# The Romantic Poets

[13] sentimentalism: the technique to arouse emotion that exceeds the norm, usually in sympathy, sorrow, etc.

1. a.

Romantic Period

As England approached the nineteenth century, sweeping social changes were well underway. The Industrial Revolution put into motion a shift of population from rural to urban areas. Parliament encouraged this process by enacting laws that forced landowners to fence in their farms. Up until this time, farmers were allowed to use community property, especially for grazing. Thus, a small farmer could make a good living, although he had little land of his own. Once the Enclosure Laws were enacted, however, small farmers were forced to close down and move to the factories in the city for their livelihood. The cities bulged with great slums, where the laborers, who worked in horrible circumstances, returned home to nightmarish conditions. Government was slow to respond, so the impetus for change was driven by the upper class Men of Letters, including Wordsworth, Coleridge, Blake, Keats, and others.

Parallel with the shifting social environment was a shift in thought. Eighteenth century thinkers did not trust information that was not obtained first hand. They felt that the senses gathered information, and one's power of reason evaluated the data. By 1800, however, some philosophers said that the mind could go beyond reason and grasp things intuitively. Thus, there were spiritual and emotional sides of man that had their places alongside our reason. The poets and novelists, as well as other artists, began to place more emphasis on the spiritual and emotional. This, and other changes in the content and style of the arts, came to be called **romanticism**.

Sometimes the emotional emphasis was self-indulgent. The new freedom to explore the emotions resulted in occasionally wallowing in them. This sentimentalism[13], as it is now called, had little merit; but a mellower side had a positive effect. Humanitarians made great strides in this period. Poets, novelists, and a few other socially influential citizens began to focus attention on the plight of the laborers for industry. They influenced politicians and eventually changed laws to protect workers and improve social problems. Thus, the "Man of Letters," as he was called, felt an obligation to touch the social conscience of his readers, and we should keep this in mind as we examine the literature from this period.

Partly due to the shocking effects of industrialism, and most certainly influenced by the French and German philosophers, a return to nature surfaced during this time. **Primitivism**, as we now label it, was derived from the belief that people are born with a natural inclination to be good; therefore, we are naturally inclined toward God. In time, however, as society imposes more of its evils on the individual, he becomes jaded and his natural tendencies are suppressed. By returning to nature, it was thought, a person could get away from the unnatural teachings of society and get back to God. Since God is found in nature, then a return to nature could restore our innate goodness. A side effect of this was the idea of the noble savage, whose supposed natural communion with God was never cut off by the trappings of society.

b. Read some poetry by Samuel Taylor Coleridge or William Wordsworth.

2. a. Although some writers were already breaking away from the conventions of the eighteenth century, Wordsworth and Coleridge not only broke away in their poems, but decided their position in the "Preface," an opening to their small volume *Lyrical Ballads, with a Few Other Poems*. *Lyrical Ballads*, first published in 1798, consisted of poems by Wordsworth and Coleridge. The poems were not enthusiastically received, so the poets reissued them in 1800 with an expanded "Preface," in which Wordsworth explained the variations found in the *Lyrical Ballads.*

Among other things, Wordsworth declared a departure in the form, content, and language of poetry. He felt that the traditional language of poetry was too artificial and needed to be toned down. He advocated a choice of words that would clearly communicate the poet's thoughts. Wordsworth resisted the idea that poetry should consist of flowery language, which had been in vogue for the past hundred years. Secondly, Wordsworth stated that the subject matter for poetry was too restrictive and needed to be expanded to include "incidents and situations from common life." This directly opposed the previously held notion that subject matter for poetry should be taken from philosophy, religion, or some other highly intellectual and moral plane. Thirdly, Wordsworth's *Lyrical Ballads* did not all rhyme. He stated that rhyme is not an essential component of poetry. Whereas many of Wordsworth's poems do rhyme, his longer works are mostly written in **blank verse**, which is unrhymed iambic pentameter.

b. Poet's Corner

**William Wordsworth** was born on April 7, 1770, in Cockermouth near the Lake District that inspired much of his writing. He was one of five children, a son of an attorney. When his mother died, his father sent the children off to school. Young Wordsworth was sadly separated from his dear sister, Dorothy, for several years, but was later reunited. He and his brothers were sent to school and boarded with Anne Tyson, who influenced his life by bringing stability and also encouraged his appreciation for natural beauty. Wordsworth's father died when he was thirteen, and he was left in the care of his uncle. He suffered with financial difficulties for most of his early years. It was not until an ailing friend died and left him a sum of money to work on his poetry that his life took a turn. Shortly afterwards, Wordsworth met Coleridge, and the effect of that meeting is evidenced in much of their poetry. Wordsworth died on April 23, 1850.

c. Read Wordsworth's poem, "Daffodils," on page 53 of *The Mentor Book of Major British Poets*.

d. In which stanza does Wordsworth tell us about his original moment of joy? When does he express the "emotion recollected in tranquillity"?

e. Based on what you have read in Days 1 and 2, what would Wordsworth hope to accomplish by sending this poem to a wealthy industrialist of his time? Write one or two paragraphs explaining your answer.

3. a. Read Wordsworth's poem, "The World Is Too Much with Us," on page 68. To review just a little, this poem is a

**sonnet**. Sonnets consist of fourteen lines and can be categorized by their rhyme schemes. This particular sonnet is a **Petrarchan sonnet** or **Classical**, which has a rhyme scheme of **abbaabba** in the **octave** (the first eight lines), and either **cdcdcd** or **cdecde** in the **sestet** (the last six lines). The octave provides a subject and the sestet provides a different look at the same subject, but the two points of view are complementary. The Shakespearean sonnet differs in that the first twelve lines consist of three distinct **quatrains** (four lines) which generally provide three different points of view on a theme. The remaining two lines tie the three points together. Shakespearean sonnets rhyme in the pattern **abab cdcd efef gg**. There are other kinds of sonnets, and variations on sonnets are numerous, but the Petrarchan and Shakespearean sonnets are very popular and typical of this form.

b. What does Wordsworth mean by "The world" in line 1?

c. What aspect of the world does line 2 show us?

d. What is the "sordid boon" in line 4?

e. How would you summarize the meaning of lines 4-8?

f. Who are Proteus and Triton? What do they represent?

g. Why does Wordsworth say he would "rather be Pagan"? (Review primitivism from **1a**.)

4\. a. Make a list of ways in which you battle the world and its attractions. Then, go back over your list and identify specific areas of influence that you feel are undesirable. For example, you might list television as a worldly influence. This doesn't say much. Under television, you might put something like this: The other night, I stayed up to watch a movie. It was just an old movie I had seen before, but I stayed up too late and felt sluggish the next day. I kept getting into arguments because I was cranky and didn't feel like doing my schoolwork or my daily chores. Although the movie was a good one, the commercials advertised an upcoming horror movie. Even now, the scenes that were shown pop into my mind when I am trying to study or just relax.

b. If you feel peer pressure, what are you being pressured to do that you know you shouldn't? What are you going to do about it? Discuss this with your teacher.

c. What advice does the Bible give about resisting the world? How do fellow Christians help you resist the world? Write one or two paragraphs explaining this.

5. a. Define the following terms. (You may refer to the *Literary Terms* found in the back of this book.) Locate examples of each using *The Mentor Book of Major British Poets* or another poetry book of your choice.

   1) blank verse
   2) Petrarchan sonnet

   b. Write a poem. Perhaps the list you wrote in **4a** will help you with topic ideas.

2.

d. Stanza three tells us about the original moment of joy.

In stanzas one and two, Wordsworth tells us what he sees. In stanza three, he tells us how he feels. Stanza four, obviously, is the recollection of the moment.

e. Wordsworth felt that industrialization created so much suffering due to the failure of wealthy factory owners to sympathize with the laborers. He thought industrialists needed to have their senses returned and brought in line to perceive God. Since industrial magnates were unlikely to absorb nature as Wordsworth did, Wordsworth thought that poems about seeing God in nature could stimulate a similar response in them without actually being in nature. Therefore, he hoped to stimulate the factory owner's conscience by leading him through an experience in which God was perceived in nature. To Wordsworth and Coleridge, enough poetry of this kind could reawaken one's spiritual side and stimulate one's God-given conscience to respond to the human suffering with kindness.

3.

b. He means much the same as the Bible does when using the term - that which indulges the flesh and keeps us from spiritual growth.

c. It shows materialism.

d. A boon is a benefit or a blessing of sorts. A sordid boon, then, appears to be a benefit, but it comes with consequences that are unfavorable.

e. Lines 4-7 provide images from nature. Line 8 tells us that we are out of tune with nature.

f. Proteus and Triton are Greek gods of the sea. They represent oneness with nature in this poem.

g. It was thought that primitive people were naturally in tune with nature because they weren't corrupted by materialism and social position, etc.

4.

b. Allow for discussion.

c. Suggestions: James 4:7, I John 2:15-16, Romans 12:2, I Peter 5:8-9

5.

a.

1) blank verse - unrhymed iambic pentameter
2) Petrarchan sonnet - poetry consisting of an octave usually with a rhyme scheme

1. a. Read Wordsworth's poem, "Lines Composed a Few Miles Above Tintern Abbey," on page 74, commonly called "Tintern Abbey." Read the poem carefully. There are three substantial indentations dividing the poem into four sections. Read each section several times, if necessary, until you understand it. Then, do the same for the next section, etc.

   Note: The friend he mentions in section four is his sister, Dorothy, who was a great source of encouragement to him.

   b. Look up any words you don't know: abbey, copse, sublime, affection, corporeal, cataract, suffer.

   c. Begin writing poetry today. You will have time the next two days to complete it.

2. a. Knowing what you do of Wordsworth, what do you think he is experiencing in section one?

   b. At the close of section one, Wordsworth mentions a Hermit. How does the Hermit fit in at this point?

   c. In general, what is section two all about?

   d. From the first nine lines of section two, identify three positive effects that recollections of moments of joy in nature can have on the individual.

   e. Work on your poem if necessary.

3. a. According to the poem, what effect does this have on a person's attitude toward other people?

   b. What is the gift Wordsworth refers to in line 15 of section two?

   c. Section three divides itself into two main parts—what he felt at Tintern Abbey as a youth and what he feels now. What is the difference?

   d. Section four, a prayer for Dorothy, enlarges upon themes already presented in the first three segments. As you read section four, ask yourself if there are any Christian sentiments in this section. Do you think Wordsworth was a Christian? Support your answer with evidence from the poem.

e. Work on your poem if necessary.

4. a. Poet's Corner

**Samuel Taylor Coleridge** was born in Ottery St. Mary, Devonshire, on October 21, 1772. He was the youngest of ten children and was a voracious reader. At nine years old, his father died, and he was sent away to school. When 'Col' was around twenty years old, he became ill and took laudanum (an opium and alcohol mixture) to relieve his pain. This began his lifelong addiction to opium, which caused him great hardships throughout his life. His meeting with Wordsworth, as mentioned earlier, was the major influence in the romantic period. Coleridge died on July 25, 1834.

b. Coleridge's best poems were, according to him, written by the Imagination about the Imagination. His purpose was to stimulate the Imagination of that materialistic, superficial group who lorded it over their employees. Whereas Wordsworth chose to do this through nature, Coleridge chose to do so through the Imagination. (The Imagination will be further discussed in Lesson 8, **3a.)**

It has been said that "The Rime of the Ancient Mariner" has been responsible for more resistance to poetry than any other single poem. This may or may not be true, but the poem seems to be little understood. Perhaps this is because it is full of medieval symbolism, which Coleridge found applicable to his purposes. Let me get you started before you read the poem, so you can get somewhat of a grasp of it before you look closely at it.

c. In stanza one, the Mariner is described as an *It*. This signifies an inhuman quality and perhaps a bad spirit. His "glittering eye" reinforces this, suggesting a hypnotic, other-worldly effect. The fact that the Mariner selected one of three people means that the one selected has been chosen because of his spiritual condition.

From medieval lore, Coleridge borrowed the homuncular and the corpuscular spirit. The homuncular spirit resides behind our eyes. It can leave the body during sleep and is vulnerable to being snared. Hair is a common snare, and we notice that the ancient Mariner has a long gray beard. Furthermore, the evil eye can fascinate and incapacitate your homuncular spirit. The corpuscular spirit lives in the blood and likes to stay in the left elbow. As you might expect, the vampire is the enemy of the corpuscular spirit.

Notice, in stanza two, that the wedding guest is concerned about the food and the fun, but not about the noble aspects of the wedding. He is in danger of losing his Imagination in favor of worldly pursuits. Nevertheless, stanza three shows us that the guest's Imagination is still working. As the poem continues, the struggle for the wedding guest's spirit continues. As the wedding guest's Imagination keeps working, Coleridge hopes that your Imagination will be working as well.

d. Read "The Rime of the Ancient Mariner," pp. 107-111, Parts I and II on your own. The story line should be rather easy to follow.

e. At what point do things start to go badly for the Mariner and his crew?

f. When do conditions begin to look more favorable for the sailors?

g. If the sailors welcomed the albatross as a sign from God, why did the Mariner shoot him?

h. Although the fog lifts when the albatross dies, what shows us, in Part II, stanza one, that this is not a good sign?

i. What happens in stanza four to make things worse?

j. Identify at least five things from the last six stanzas of Part II that show us a metaphoric picture of Hades.

5. a. Continue in your reading of "The Rime of the Ancient Mariner," Parts III and IV, pp. 111-115.

b. What kind of visitors approach the Mariner's ship?

c. Read stanza eleven again. What specific kind of evil being is the woman?

d. The last four stanzas of Part IV are transitional. Are the watersnakes good or evil?

e. Why does the albatross fall from the Mariner's neck?

1.

b. abbey - a monastery or nunnery
copse - a thicket of bushes
sublime - majestic
corporeal - bodily; tangible
cataract - a large waterfall or downpour
suffer - to permit

2.

a. He is having a moment of joy in which he feels in tune with nature and close to God.

b. The Hermit has abandoned the worldly society of England and secluded himself where he is continually in touch with nature. Wordsworth is saying that the Hermit is to be more admired than a wealthy industrialist.

c. Section two is about the recollection of the moment of joy and the power of the recollections to revive the spirit.

d. Lines 4, 5, and 6 of section two identify loneliness, the din of cities, and weariness as conditions which can be remedied by getting in tune with nature.

3.

a. We are encouraged to be kind and loving and to demonstrate this by our actions.

b. When we are in tune with nature, we see beyond nature and recognize the spirit behind it. This reveals that we are in touch with that spirit.

c. As a youngster, he was in touch with nature without really understanding it. He simply felt the thrill of nature spontaneously. As an adult, Wordsworth has had time to experience the world's influence. He now realizes the value of nature to keep him from being dragged down by the world. Furthermore, he understands the spirit behind nature and is able to appreciate it.

d. It is obvious that Wordsworth knew a good deal about Christianity because of the values he embraced, because he saw God in nature (Romans 1), and because he recognized his need for spiritual impartation to help him behave well. However, Wordsworth never says that Christ is the way to the Father. Ultimately, it is doubtful that he was a Christian in the born again sense. He probably thought he was a Christian, having been raised in a Christian culture.

4.

e. A fierce storm blows them far off toward the South Pole.

f. After the albatross appears, a favorable wind comes up.

g. The Mariner is in strange, perilous seas. The albatross, likewise, is out of his element and eats strange foods and flies around the ship, giving the Mariner weird impressions. If the Mariner's Imagination were working, he would ignore everything confusing him and concentrate on the Godsend. However, he disregards his

Imagination and acts out of his Fancy. If you answered that the Mariner lost his Imagination for a moment, that is what Coleridge wanted you to see. As for my explanation for this answer, you aren't expected to see that on your own.

h. The sun rises in the west and sets in the east. The world has turned upside down for the sailors.

i. The men acknowledge that it was right to shoot the albatross. Now they are all guilty.

j.

1) It is very hot, but there is no water.
2) The sea has become a sea of rot.
3) The sea is slimy.
4) There are slimy creatures all around.
5) There are death fires.
6) The water is like witch's oils.
7) A bad spirit lurks under the sea.
8) They are so thirsty that their tongues are withered.
9) The Mariner is punished by the continued reminder of his crime hung about his neck.

5.

b. Evil spirits approach the Mariner's ship.

c. She is a vampire, capable of taking the corpuscular spirit.

d. Although serpents are traditionally evil, the Mariner sees the watersnakes for what they really are — just snakes. They are God's creatures, just like any other animal.

e. He is able to bless the snakes, indicating that his spirit is being restored. This is confirmed by his ability to pray. Although the Mariner has been through a great trial, he is beginning to use his Imagination again.

1. a. Continue in your reading of "The Rime of the Ancient Mariner," Parts V and VI, pp. 115-121. Pay attention to the marginal notes to help you follow the events.

   b. What do the rain and wind symbolize?

   c. What do the words *shrieve*, *rood*, and *kirk* mean?

   d. Has the Mariner's spirit been restored by the end of Part V?

   e. The spell is broken in stanza ten of Part VI. From this point to the end of this section, state in your own words the main points of the story line.

   f. Begin writing poetry today. Include figurative language: metaphor, simile, personification. You will have time the next two days to complete your poem.

2. a. Read Part VII of "The Rime of the Ancient Mariner," pp. 121-124.

   b. Given what you know of Wordsworth, what do you think the spiritual condition of the Hermit is?

   c. Why has the Hermit come to see the Mariner?

   d. Continue working on your poem, if necessary.

3. a. A brief glance at the philosophy of Wordsworth and Coleridge is helpful in understanding their poetry. Taking from the philosophy of Keats and others, they formed a theory that Coleridge expressed in Chapter 14 of his *Biographia Literia*. Simply put, one gathers data through the senses, and this data is sent to a part of the intellect called the Fancy. The Fancy is mechanical, like a computer, and incapable of creating ideas. Next, the organized material goes to the Imagination. First, the Primary Imagination analyzes the data regarding its moral implications (whether or not action should be taken, etc.). The Secondary Imagination, however, is the highest faculty of our minds. It is here that creativity exists and ideas are formed. Also, the Secondary Imagination is where the mind can intuitively come in touch with God.

The thrust of Wordsworth and Coleridge's poetry was to stimulate the Imagination. They felt that modern industrialists were operating by the Fancy, and needed their moral and spiritual levels regenerated. They wrote poetry to do this, but they went in different directions. Coleridge wrote poems about the Imagination intended to open the Imagination. Wordsworth saw God in nature. He felt that poems about his own revelations of God in nature would stimulate others to see Him in nature. This is why Wordsworth is called the nature poet.

Wordsworth's theory of creativity is closely tied to his philosophy. When Wordsworth had moments of ecstasy when he saw God in nature, the emotion was overwhelming to him. He felt that he could not write in this emotional state, and he would wait until his emotions subsided. Then, he would reflect on his experience and regenerate a feeling similar to the original. Wordsworth called this reflective process "emotion recollected in tranquillity." It was in this state of vivid imagination that he felt he accomplished his best writing and that he communicated a moment's perception of God.

b. Read Coleridge's poem, "Kubla Khan," page 79, and his note on page 78. Read the poem several times and try to trace the path of the river Alph.

c. Continue working on your poem, if necessary.

4. Do a little research today and find out about Kubla Khan. Who was he? Where and when did he live? What did he accomplish, etc.?

5. a. Let's say that Alph (Alpha, the beginning) is a symbol for the spiritual world, and the dome represents the human mind, according to Coleridge. Notice all the elaborate imagery in the first stanza. What process is the mind working in?

b. The information gathered through the senses is sent to the Fancy. At what point, on page 79, do we know that the Imagination begins to work?

c. At what point do we know that we are in stage two of the Imagination, where we can sense the spirit of God?

d. In the last stanza, what do you think Coleridge is saying?

1.
b. The rain and wind symbolize God.

c. shrieve - minister the sacrament of penance
rood - cross symbolizing the cross of Christ
kirk - church

d. Not yet. He hasn't yet shown that he has either learned his lesson or that he is functioning with his Imagination. However, he is getting there.

e. A refreshing wind comes up and blows the ship. Since the sea is calm, the wind is a Godsend. The wind steers the Mariner toward his home. As the boat approaches home, the angels leave the dead crewmen. Next, a boat approaches with a pilot, the pilot's son, and a Hermit. Note that the hermit is a holy man.

2.
b. He lives in the woods, close to nature and away from society; therefore, he is somewhat of a holy man.

c. The Hermit's presence reveals to the Mariner what form his penance shall take.

4. Some helpful information: Kubla(i) Khan (1215-1294) was the grandson of Mongol warrior, Genghis Khan. Whereas his grandfather is remembered as a great conqueror, Kubla Khan is credited for his role in bringing order and agriculture to the conquered territory. He brought the unification of China, establishing the Mongol Dynasty. He founded the capital city in Cambaluc, now Beijing. His lavishly splendid lifestyle and the poor management of his successors slowly led to the destruction of the Mongol dynasty.

5.
a. You can see the gardens, etc., and hear the rills (brooks), as well as smell the incense-bearing trees and feel the sunny spots. We are at the stage of gathering information through the senses.

b. We know that the Imagination begins to work when the river is "flowing up."

c. We know at the point when the prophecy occurs (last line, page 79). A prophecy cannot come through the rational mind but must come by the spirit.

d. He is saying that his job is to give poems of the Imagination to those who need it. That is the reason for this poem.

# Frankenstein,
# or,
# The Modern Prometheus

**Teacher's Note: The beginning of this lesson includes a summary of the novel. This is designed to help you discuss the novel with the student. Also, some students are better able to understand the novel if they read a summary; however, it should not replace reading the full novel. Please note that any surprise element or suspense is revealed in the summary. Use the summary to best meet your student's needs.**

Lessons 9-12 Novel Unit-*Frankenstein, or, The Modern Prometheus* by Mary Shelley
Published by Bantam Books ISBN 0-553-21247-8 (or any edition of the 1818 publication)

1. a. Link to the Author: Mary Shelley

Mary Shelley was born on August 30, 1797, in London, England. Her parents were freethinking radicals; their home was often visited by philosophers, poets, and writers. Among these visitors was the romantic poet, Percy Bysshe Shelley, whom she ran away with at the age of 16. Mary's own life was similar to a Gothic tale filled with tragedies; one tragedy was the death of her husband Percy when she was only twenty-four. Though often overlooked as a literary figure during the romantic era, her novel, *Frankenstein*, remains today a classic. Despite many suitors, Mary chose to remain a widow until her death in 1851.

b. Note: In Mary Shelley's *Frankenstein*, the original telling of the story, one will not find a hunchbacked sidekick, nor grisly details of body parts and desecrated graves, nor great detail of bizarre, futuristic scientific equipment. In fact, also missing is "Dr. Frankenstein" himself; Victor Frankenstein was a student when he created the creature. Young Victor claims to have philanthropic intentions; he is certainly no mad scientist. Further inaccuracies in the celluloid versions include the personage of the creature. He is nothing of the slow-witted, creaking, ponderous fellow of movie fame; instead, he speaks eloquently and pointedly. This synthesis of monstrosity and intellect instill in the reader a much wider array of feelings towards the monster than simply fear or disgust. While such obtuse details may make for popular filmography, they utterly diminish the entire point of Shelley's great work. If you have ever seen any of the movies made about the monster, forget them now. You are about to read the original, the story as it was meant to be known, a story chilling in its possibilities and its indictments.

It is interesting to note that the idea for this story arose from a ghost story contest, in which her husband and the poet, Lord Byron, were among the participants. The game took place during vacation in the Swiss Alps, a truly sublime arena for what must have been as eloquent and imaginative a storytelling contest as any in history. While the others' efforts soon dissipated into the mountain air, Shelley's mind quickly formed her masterpiece with the very zeal, fervor, and celerity that the young Victor (Frankenstein) formed his.

Summary of *Frankenstein, or, The Modern Prometheus*

The story begins as Robert Walton writes to his sister about his expedition to the Arctic. He describes how he and his crew came upon the discovery of a man near death. This man is Victor Frankenstein, and he begins his tale.

Victor was born into a privileged class. He attends the University of Ingolstadt where his life is deeply affected by M. Waldman, a professor who encourages him to study modern science. Not as a madman, but as a benefactor of mankind, Victor hopes to discover a way to overcome death and create life. He begins his intense studies and eventually withdraws from his friends and family into his laboratory. Finally, after two years, he completes his experiments with body parts of cadavers and "successfully" creates life in a hideous form. Quickly, Victor realizes the horror of his deeds. He rejects his creation and flees. Victor becomes ill and for two years is unknowing of the creature's whereabouts. He hears news about the murder of William, his beloved, younger brother. Immediately, Victor knows that his creation is the murderer. However, the townspeople quickly accuse Justine, an orphan who lives with the Frankenstein family, as the murderer, and she is quickly hanged. Victor now holds himself responsible for two deaths.

Frankenstein meets his creature in the mountains where the creature tells him his plight. The creature had spent the last two years observing some poor cottagers and taught himself to speak and read. By reading Frankenstein's journal, which he found, he discovers the truth about his existence. He now feels rejected not only by strangers but his own creator, his own "father." The creature begs Frankenstein to create a companion for him, someone "horrible" like himself, who would not reject him. The creature promises that he and his bride will flee civilization to never to be seen again. Victor finally agrees and creates a new monster. Upon completion, he questions what he has done and destroys his creation. Frankenstein's creature curses him and vows vengeance. Shortly, Henry Clerval, his best friend, is killed and later, on Victor's wedding night, Elizabeth, his bride, is also killed. Frankenstein is distraught and determines to follow the creature until he is destroyed.

Frankenstein's pursuits lead him to the Arctic, where he meets up with Walton. After telling his tale, Frankenstein dies. Soon thereafter, the creature is discovered by the side of the deceased and wails, "Farewell...my spirit will sleep in peace...farewell!" He jumps out the window to be lost to the icy waves.

c. Major characters in *Frankenstein*:

Robert Walton: an explorer on an expedition in the Arctic
Victor Frankenstein: the creator of the "monster"
William Frankenstein: Victor's youngest brother
Justine Moritz: an orphan girl who lives with the Frankensteins
Henry Clerval: Victor's close friend
Elizabeth Lavenza: an orphan girl whom the Frankensteins adopt; Victor's bride-to-be
M. Waldman: the professor who urges Victor to study modern science
Frankenstein's "monster": Victor's creation

d. In reading stories and novels, one should always try to look for themes or main ideas woven throughout the story. A theme may be as simple as the beauty and power of nature, or more complex, such as one character's transgression of natural law. *Frankenstein*, by Mary Shelley, has both of these themes and others.

Begin today by reading Letters 1-4 of Shelley's *Frankenstein*.

e. Letter 1
To whom is Robert Walton writing?

f. What seems to be Walton's motivation in his exploration?

g. Letter 2
What does Walton feel is missing in his life?
Note the allusion Walton makes to Coleridge's "The Rime of the Ancient Mariner."

h. Letters 3 and 4
What predicament does Walton and his crew find themselves in late July?

i. Describe the three major events that occur within hours of each other.

j. Despite his enfeebled condition, what does the stranger ask of his rescuers before allowing himself to be drawn into the ship?

k. What soon becomes Walton's impression of the stranger?

l. Although we don't know what has happened to the stranger, what does he say about his life?

m. Walton's regard for the stranger increases magnanimously over the days and weeks that follow, to the extent where he, at one point, refers to the stranger as a "divine wanderer." Why do you think he holds the man in such high revere?

Note: When reading stories with narrators within the action, be aware that the narrators are not necessarily entirely reliable. With Walton's letters to his sister, Shelley has created a framework narrative for the novel. Note that at the end of the fourth letter, we have a second narrator.

2. a. Read Chapters 1-2.

b. Chapters 1 & 2
Find Geneva on a world map. Note its geographical relationships with surrounding countries.

c. Give brief descriptions of Elizabeth Lavenza, Henry Clerval, and young Victor [Frankenstein].

d. Reread the final paragraph of Chapter 2. Are you willing to accept Victor Frankenstein's portrayal of his childhood?

e. Chapter 3
Although he knows natural philosophers like Magnus and Paracelsus to be of little worth, why does Victor still prefer these writers to modern philosophers?

f. What changes Victor's mind?

3. a. Read Chapters 4-5.

b. Chapter 4
What is the abrupt change in Victor's manner once he begins his studies at Ingolstadt?

c. Why does Victor intensively study physiology—a practice that, in his words, is "irksome and almost intolerable"?

d. Since we already know the final result of Victor's discovery (from his own words, "destruction and infallible misery"), what general, predominant conflict do you predict for this novel? (e.g., Man vs. Man, Man vs. Self, etc.)

e. What do you think is the driving force behind Victor's endeavors?

f. How does Victor feel, in retrospect, of his frenzied scientific pursuits?

g. Chapter 5
How does Victor's attitude towards his creation change?

h. How does Henry Clerval assist Victor? What does he give up for his friend?

4. a. Read Chapters 6-8.

b. Chapter 6
Give some differences between Henry and Victor.

c. What effect does Henry have on Victor?

d. Chapter 7
Make sure that you are keeping track of the time throughout the story. How much time has passed since Victor's

experiment came to horrible fruition and his reception of his father's letter informing him of William's death?

e. As you read this novel, make a note of Victor's extreme, almost oblivious, arrogance. Give a few examples of this so far.

f. When Victor sees the creature during the storm, what are his immediate assumptions regarding this brother and the creature's actions? What do you think of these assumptions?

g. What action does Victor take when he hears that Justine has been arrested for the murder of William? Explain his actions.

h. Chapter 8
What is the evidence against Justine?

i. What are your thoughts regarding Victor's reaction to the conviction?

5. Write one or two paragraphs explaining why you think Victor feels the way he does about the creature. Are his feelings rational or irrational, well founded or unfounded? Try to place yourself in Victor's position and imagine how you might respond to the situation.

1.

e. He is writing to his sister.

f. His trend of thought is heroic conquest and discovery- to discover mysteries of the natural world (e.g., a path through the pole, or understanding of the magnetic forces of the earth's poles).

g. He feels he is missing a friend who can empathize with his dreams and desires.

h. The ice surrounds the ship, threatening to crush her.

i. The crew sees a giant, savage figure riding a dog-drawn sledge, speeding across the ice. This leads the men to believe that they are closer to land than they had thought. A few hours later, the ice breaks up, freeing the ship. The next morning they rescue an emaciated European man from an ice floe.

j. He asks in which direction they are sailing.

k. He believes the man to be a noble benevolent man, even despite the suffering that has desecrated his body and spirit. Walton has, in fact, found a "friend on the wide ocean."

l. He says, "I have lost everything, and cannot begin life anew."

m. It is certainly possible that the stranger is everything that Walton claims he is. But it is just as possible that because Walton has been without suitable company (recall his definition of a true friend and the painful lack thereof on board the ship), he has overcompensated in his relationship with the stranger.

2.

c. Elizabeth is Victor's adopted sister. She is, in all respects, affectionate and acquiescent, graceful and beautiful, and according to Victor, a perfect angel.

Henry is Victor's best friend, much like a brother. His sole talent and interest revolves around writing and literature. Victor is the son of a wealthy, political Genevese family. He recalls his childhood as his halcyon days, "before misfortune had tainted (his) mind." As a young boy, he was extremely well read in natural philosophy and in the writings of centuries old natural scientists. He later learned Greek, English, and German and was interested in mathematics.

d. Answers may vary.

e. He believes that the science of his day has lost its penchant or grandeur and omnipotence. Certainly, men who sought to turn ordinary metals into gold (the alchemists) were more appealing romantically and more grandiose than those who sought to debunk them.

f. He attends M. Waldman's lecture on chemistry. Waldman reveals the miracles that modern science is producing, thereby inspiring Victor to examine modern chemistry.

3.

b. Previously, we saw his unerring devotion to his family and his dolor at leaving them. But during the first two years at the university, he does not visit his family once.

c. He is "animated by an almost supernatural enthusiasm." Later in the chapter, we see that his work is "urged on by an eagerness which perpetually increased" and has "taken an irresistible hold on [his] imagination."

d. At this point, it seems that Victor is dabbling in a forbidden science, an application reserved for God—the creation of life. So, one might predict that the impetus of the novel will stem from the conflict between God/Nature vs. Man. Note the broad similarity between this novel and the biblical story of Babel.

e. It is his insatiable hunger for knowledge.

f. He tells Walton that any endeavor, should it cause you to neglect simple, God-given pleasures of life, is "unlawful" and "not befitting the human mind." This adjuration to attend to the pure, natural aspects of life can also be found in the writings of Shelley's contemporary romantics, as in Wordsworth's "Tintern Abbey" or in John Keats' "Ode to a Nightingale."

g. When the creature comes to life, Victor sees living, pulsating features making up an animate being out of what was once only cold, unfeeling scraps upon a dissecting table. The psychological metamorphosis is overwhelming.

h. He nurses Victor for several months, without telling Victor's family of the magnitude of the illness so as to protect them from the potentially devastating news.

In caring for Victor, he gives up his own studies.

4.

b. Victor is a student of natural philosophy and science. He becomes so consumed in his studies that he neglects to even write to his family.

Henry is a student of languages and literature. He neglects his studies to care for his friend. (Henry is the measuring stick against Victor.)

c. Victor recounts to Walton how his friend's love and consideration soon restored his spirits until he became "the same happy creature" of his childhood.

d. About a year and a half have passed.

e. Possible answers:
1) He fails to consider the feelings of his family as he works relentlessly at the university.
2) He states that during his studies in physiology, he was propelled by an "almost supernatural" force, as if it was his divine calling to

understand the miracle of life and then create it. We soon learn that he has violated nature, not obeyed it.
3) While he works on his experiment, he fantasizes of legions of his own creations calling him master, praising him. He becomes quite power-hungry.
4) When he learns of his brother's death, he refers to the occurrence as "my misfortune."

f. He quickly assumes that the creature is his brother's murderer and wonders if this "depraved wretch, whose delight was in carnage and misery" was responsible for more evil.

This is not a reasonable supposition or description of a creature he has not seen for more than a few moments.

g. He does nothing, assuming that since Justine is innocent, no evidence will be brought against her.

Again, Victor does not take responsibility for his actions. (Keep in mind that he believes that his creation is responsible for the murder.) He allows Justine to suffer in jail rather than tell his story. He was entirely prepared to let his family know about the creature—he referred to him wildly to Ernest, but when he realizes that he can get away without incriminating the creature (and himself), he becomes quiet.

h. She had a poor alibi for her whereabouts at the time the crime was committed. She was seen post hoc near the scene of the crime. The locket and picture that William had been wearing were found in her clothing. The likelihood of a setup was lessened due to the fact that the supposed true villain had left the valuable jewelry with Justine—the jewelry being the apparent motive for the crime.

i. He still had a chance to save the girl. Even though his story may have sounded rather fantastic, it was a chance to save her life. Instead, he only broods over his own misfortune.
He even says that Justine herself "felt not as I did, such deep and bitter agony." Instead of choosing to save Justine, Victor chooses self-pity and arrogance.

1. a. Read Chapters 9-10 of Mary Shelley's *Frankenstein.*

   b. Chapter 9
   We have already discussed what appears to be a rather severe overreaction by Victor regarding the disposition of the creature. In this chapter, Victor tells Walton of his surpassing hatred and loathing for the creature. Why do you think Victor feels so strongly toward a creature he has seen only a few times for brief seconds?

   c. How has the death of Justine (and William earlier) affected Victor, Elizabeth, and the father?

   d. Chapter 10
   Once more, note Shelley's attention and reverence to the beauty and majesty of nature. How does this affect Victor? What does the power of mountain, as described by Victor, symbolize?

   e. Describe Victor's (Shelley's) thoughts on the "sensibilities" of man. What do you think of this philosophy?

   f. Describe the creature's approach over the treacherous terrain.

   g. What does the creature say of Victor's threat to kill him? What does the creature mean by, "How dare you sport thus with life?"

   h. This initial encounter between the two, creator and creation, is remarkable for its reversal of roles. Have the two acted as you might have expected?

   i. Recall Victor's short recitation on mutability and his thoughts on the inconstancy of man earlier in the chapter. How does Victor himself fulfill his criticism of his fellow man?

2. a. Read Chapters 11-12.

   b. Chapter 11
   How was the creature treated in his first encounters with man?

c. Describe the home he creates for himself.

d. Write a physical description of the creature based on the reactions he receives in the story.

e. Chapter 12
Give a brief description of the cottagers. How does their virtue affect the creature?

f. How does the creature react to seeing his reflection in the pool of water?

g. What are the creature's hopes for himself and the family?

3. a. Read Chapters 13-14.

b. Chapters 13-14
How did the creature learn not only the words and the grammar of the family, but also a cursory amount of ancient history?

c. In learning about governments and social classes, genders and families, what does the creature discern about his own position in the world of man?

4. a. Read Chapters 15-16.

b. Chapter 15
What are the three books the creature finds? What does the creature learn from these?

c. How does the creature finally become acquainted with his maker?

d. What plans does the creature make to introduce himself to the family? Describe the ensuing scene.

e. Chapter 16
What does the creature plan the next day, and how are these plans thwarted?

f. Describe the paradox of sorts of the creature's feelings for his maker.

g. Why does the creature first approach William? What are the creature's intentions after he learns who the boy is?

h. How is Justine Moritz's earlier entrapment explained here?

i. Chapter 17
What are the creature's arguments for the creation of a mate? What are Victor's arguments?

5. The creature marvels at Victor's ever-changing conviction regarding the creation of a mate, but the creature himself is as inconstant as Victor. Based on what you have read about the creature's personality, would you trust him to hold to his promise? Write one or two paragraphs describing the psychological processes that have been at work within the creature. Recall his many changes in mood over the last few chapters. How might these shape or reshape his personality? Whether or not you feel that the creature is trustworthy, give evidence from the story to back up your claim. In your explanation, keep in mind the theme of mutability.

1.

b. Perhaps Victor subconsciously feels that he has broken natural (divine) law with his creation and work. This may have lead him to develop a fierce animosity so rapidly.

c. Victor descends into a deep, brooding depression. He cannot face his family and contemplates suicide.

Elizabeth now begins to doubt the inherent goodness in man and in life. She goes about her affairs soberly and without enjoyment.

Victor's father grieves quietly, attempting to carry his despondent family, but his physical health begins to suffer.

d. It seems to be the one thing that affords him any solace. Indeed, he is wholly captivated and his mind is entranced by the resplendence he sees.

Moreover, the power of Mont Blanc is representative of the omnipotence of nature. Keep in mind, this is a power he has transgressed.

e. He feels that man's higher sense of existence and sense of his surroundings are a curse, weighing on his soul and engendering him inconstant in his thoughts and actions. This capriciousness causes us to be less free than beasts in that we are bound by our inability to focus our energies on one thing. Instead, we are tossed this way and that by the slightest instigation or impulse.

f. In Victor's words, he traversed the distance with "superhuman" strength and agility.

g. He calmly acknowledges that Victor's hatred is warranted on the grounds of his hideous appearance (in perfect English, I might add) but also actually chastises Victor for abandoning him. His complaint against Victor is reasonable: Is it not wrong for a being to give life to another being but abandon it immediately? And now the creator wishes to kill the creation..., for what reason? Indeed, Victor has sported with life.

h. The creature is calm and civilized (at least in tongue), while Victor is livid with rage and disgust. He is physically violent with the creature on more than one occasion.

i. Just minutes after he bemoaned the whimsicality of man, Victor quickly goes from utter abhorrence for the creature to feeling compassion for him.

2.

b. He was met with great fear and, as a result of this, violence.

c. He discovers a tiny hut, adjacent to a small cottage. The coarse dwelling is made of wood and surrounded by a pigsty and a pool of water. He walls up the open side of it in such a way that he can readily enter and exit. He further seals up any cracks in the walls and carpets the floor with clean straw. Due to its proximity to the chimney of the cottage, his miniature house is kept fairly warm. Apparently, the little hut had been added to the cottage where a window had been, so he is able to see into the house.

d. He seems to be intolerably ugly, due to the reaction of those whom he encounters. He has been created with a gigantic stature (for practical purposes by Victor). He possesses a remarkable ability to acclimate himself to any physical condition, as evidenced by the fact that he has survived a harsh winter with little protection.

e. As it is winter, they are extremely impoverished (although the creature does not soon recognize this), but they show a strong love and generosity toward each other. Their kindness rubs off on the creature, and he discontinues his pilfering of their stores and finds his food in the forest. He also brings them firewood and is greatly pleased at their appreciation of it.

f. He is at first frightened by the monstrous form he perceives, and when he realizes that the brute is himself, he is deeply affected. After seeing his three neighbors daily, imagine his despair upon seeing himself. He begins to suspect his misplacement in this world.

g. He hopes that once he has mastered their language, he might finally introduce himself. He knows that they will be frightened initially at his grotesque appearance, but he hopes that his kindness and peaceful disposition will soon enamor them with him. As we shall see, his naivety is similar to Victor's oblivious arrogance in one respect— neither is very adept at predicting outcomes.

3.

b. He listened as they taught Safie their language through a book on the revolutions of empires.

c. He learns that wealth and social status are the two most important things to men. Combined, they afford a man all the pleasure and honor he could desire; without either, a man is rendered an outcast. But he wonders if he is even a man; physically, he differs from men in many ways. He has no recollection of parents and has never found anyone with whom to communicate. And he again wonders whether he has any role in the world at all.

4.

b. From Goethe's *The Sorrows of Young Werther*, he learns of gentility and romance and all sentimentality.

From the volume of Plutarch's *Lives*, he reads about armies and nations and cities, all climates wholly foreign to his own limited experience.

From Milton's *Paradise Lost*, he reads about another creator and creation.

c. He discovers Victor's notes in

the pocket of the coat that he has taken from the laboratory. From these, he learns of Victor's repulsion of his creation, and he first begins to curse his creator. He compares his creator with God from *Paradise Lost* and curses him all the more. He dreams of an Eve of his own and curses his creator when he awakens.

d. Knowing that his principal physical offense is his appearance, he decides to wait until the blind father, De Lacey, is alone in the cottage to make his introduction.

He knocks at the cottage door, and upon being received by the old man, begins his first conversation. The old man perceives sincerity in the creature and offers to assist him in his endeavors. However, at the critical moment in their conversation, the rest of the family returns and the creature is beaten and driven away by Felix who is attempting to defend his father.

e. He realizes that, in his desire for human companionship, he had moved too quickly. He resolves to speak with De Lacey again. However, the next day he learns that Felix has quickly sold the house and the family has moved away. He never sees them again. Frustrated and vengeful over this excruciating loss, he burns the house to the ground.

f. He hates Victor terribly for abandoning him, but he knows that Victor is his only opportunity for restitution. Victor is the only man in the world who (the creature feels) owes him something.

g. He hopes that perhaps the boy's ingenuousness has protected him from the prejudices of his elders. When the boy tells him that his father's name is Frankenstein the creature is enraged. However, the creature is unclear about whether he intended to kill the boy or intended some other harm.

h. In a rather fantastic coincidence, the creature sees Justine passing by and, in the knowledge that neither she nor any woman would ever look kindly upon him, he condemns her to death by placing the evidence in her dress pocket.

i. The creature tells Victor that the only reason he has become evil and has committed evil deeds is because he has not had anyone to empathize in his plight. With a mate, this will no longer be a problem.

Victor first tells the creature that he will surely return to the world of man to seek the acceptance he desires and when the creature counters with the argument above, Victor consents to his request.

1. a. Read Chapters 18-19 of Mary Shelley's *Frankenstein.*

   b. Chapter 18
   Compare Victor against Henry Clerval. Where are the significant differences?

   c. What do you sense from Victor's homage to Henry near the end of the chapter?

   d. Chapter 19
   Describe the essence of the difference between this creation and the former.

2. a. Read Chapters 20-21

   b. Chapter 20
   In his moment of idleness before work, what rationale does Victor use to dissuade himself from his task?

   c. What prompts Victor to destroy his work?

   d. What is the creature's threat as he leaves Victor?

   e. Chapter 21
   What is the evidence against Victor in Henry's murder?

   f. What does the murder of Henry mean to Victor? Does it have any symbolic meaning?

   g. Victor believes that "some destiny of the most horrible kind hangs over me." How do you interpret these words?

3. a. Read Chapters 22-23.

   b. Chapter 22
   What do you think of Victor's reasoning for not telling his father, or anyone else, of his creation?

   c. What is Victor's understanding of the creature's words, "I will be with you on your wedding night"? Is this the same as your understanding of the warning?

   d. What does Victor write in response to Elizabeth's letter?

   e. What is Elizabeth's disposition on the day of the wedding?

f. Chapter 23
How does Victor look upon the climax of his story? Describe the falling action of the plot.

g. Reread the section in which Victor speaks to the Genevese magistrate. What can this scenario be likened to?

4. a. Read Chapter 24.

b. What is Victor's one remaining human emotion?

c. Why does the creature tell Victor that he is satisfied?

d. What two things drive Victor in his pursuit of the creature?

e. What request does Victor make of Walton? What is his warning to Walton?

f. Is the creature treacherous? Why or why not?

g. When Walton inquires about the particulars of the creation, what does Victor tell him? How might Victor serve as a warning to Walton?

h. What is Victor's defense of his actions?

i. Why do you think the creature is upset at Victor's death? Is he sorrowful because the chase is finished (as Walton reasons) or does the creature truly feel pity for his creator?

j. Why did Mary Shelley call her novel *The Modern Prometheus*?

5. Today, you have one of two choices:

a. Find a summary and/or analysis of *Paradise Lost* on the web or at your local library. Look for similar themes between the two literary works.

OR

b. Write two to three paragraphs explaining how Shelley uses nature in her novel. What is its role? Specifically, what do Mont Blanc, snow or weather in general, etc., represent? Keep in mind the romantic conception of nature.

1.

b. Henry is practically faultless. We see in him none of the debilitating flaws found in Victor's character. His preeminent goodness is verified by his exultation of nature, by the awe inspired within him. Were it not for Henry's excellent virtue, Victor's moral decline would not be so keenly apperceived by the reader. As Victor states in the next chapter, "...in Clerval I saw the image of my former self."

c. Henry is apparently no longer alive. This casts a foreboding over the subsequent chapters.

d. In the original creation, Victor was driven by the excitement of discovery. In this second attempt, he already knows the dreadful result, and it sickens him.

2.

b. He considers the possibility that the female creature would not be bound to the agreement he and the creature had previously made. He wonders if the sight of the other will repulse them both. Furthermore, if they were to attract each other, the outcome could be a race of the creatures. (However, if Victor is truly proficient in his craft, he could surely set up a defense against that.)

c. He sees the creature looking in at the window. Victor believes he sees an evil will in his expression and, in a fit of passion, destroys his work.

d. He tells Victor that he will be with him on his wedding day.

e. One witness saw a boat offshore, much like Victor's, with a single passenger at the time of the murder. Another saw the boat leave shore an hour earlier. Due to the storm that night, it was quite possible that the same boat be driven back to the original landing hours later.

f. Henry was his greatest confidant and companion (although, even with Henry, Victor did not tell his secret). In a manner similar to Elizabeth, Henry possessed a profound delight in all things good and beautiful that inspired Victor and exhilarated him continually.

Henry's death casts an ominous gloom over Victor's future.

g. It seems that Victor senses a punishment of sorts. He later calls his impending execution "justice," acknowledging that he deserves a punishment for his actions. However, he believes to be guilty by association with the creature; his actual guilt is deeper than that. By the end of the chapter, with Victor still alive, we must wonder if justice has yet been resolved.

3.

b. He claims that he does not disclose the truth because he fears he will be thought mad, but he still tells his father, with no further explanation, that his actions have killed William, Justine, and Henry. He further claims that he would gladly have died many deaths to save them, and yet he will not seek help against the creature for fear of his own reputation.

We have discussed other such discrepancies in Victor's account of himself. As the reader, you must ask yourself how reliable Victor is as a narrator.

c. Victor views it as a threat Implied, "No." It seems clear to the reader that the creature's method of retribution is focused on mental suffering for Victor and not so much physical suffering.

d. He writes that he desires to marry her, that she is his last chance at happiness. In a fit of tactlessness, he debases the letter a bit when he tells her of a terrible secret that he must confide in her on their wedding night—a secret which "will chill your frame with horror."

e. She is uncharacteristically quiet and pensive. She anticipates Victor's secret with restrained fear.

f. The incidents following the murder of his wife are immaterial. Victor quickly and briefly narrates the events that followed Elizabeth's death—the death of his father, the death of other friends, his own subsequent malaise.

g. It is markedly similar to the scene in which the creature tells his story to Victor and requests his assistance. Note Victor's vivid anger when he suspects that the magistrate will not do as he asks. From here on out, Victor becomes the creature, the hunter.

4.

b. Victor's one remaining human emotion is revenge.

c. The creature's desire was to make Victor as miserable as possible, just as he had become. With Victor's covenant to pursue the creature until either died, the creature was assured that Victor would never again have any peace or joy in his life.

d. 1) He is driven by his vow of vengeance.
2) He is also driven by a "mechanical impulse of some power of which I was unconscious." He is driven more by this, he believes, than by his physical quest for revenge. Nature/God is still punishing him.

e. While he does not ask Walton to continue the hunt once he is dead, he does ask that, if the creature should appear before Walton, he should destroy him.

He warns Walton that the creature is persuasive, but treacherous. Although he might make a compelling argument, he adjures Walton to hear him not.

f. Answers will vary.

g. Victor calls the question one of "senseless curiosity," and asks him "to what do your questions tend?"

Walton's own quest is to reach the North Pole. Like Victor, he is driven by the desire to discover, and by the glory therein. Had Victor considered the true reason for his creation, he may have seen the uselessness of it. He dreamed of creating an army of creatures who would bend to his will. There was no inherent usefulness in that, and thus, no inherent good in it. Walton, likewise, seeks personal glory. Victor warns him of the dangers of blind pride. Indeed, Walton has brought himself and his crew very close to death. And for what? His last entreaty to Walton was to "Seek happiness in tranquility and avoid ambition."

h. He admits that he had a responsibility to the creature, as his Creator, but he believes that he had a higher obligation to the people around him — they being many, the creature being one. So, after his failure toward the creature, his only obligation left was to his fellow man. He had already failed to uphold his creation, but, in denying the creature's request, he upheld his responsibility to his fellow man.

i. Answers will vary.

j. In Greek mythology, just as Prometheus transgressed divine law by giving man fire, so did Victor overstep man's natural bounds by bestowing life at his own whim and peril. Prometheus was punished for his actions and bound to the side of the cliff, but Victor was left to deal with the consequences of his actions. Literally unbound, he was given the freedom (not afforded to Prometheus) to either correct his error or delve deeper into his iniquity.

1-5.

a. This week, you will write a compare and contrast essay on *Frankenstein*. Keep the paper to about five hundred words or about two typewritten pages, double-spaced. You have one week to complete it.

b. With your teacher's permission, view the 1931 black and white cinematic version of *Frankenstein*.

c. For obvious reasons, a film cannot cover an entire novel. Some things to consider while you are watching the movie:

1) Why do you think the film producer changed the story as he did?
2) How are the major characters different than the novel?
3) How does the plot differ?
4) How has the film moved away from Shelley's romantic style?

d. Use the following guideline when writing your compare and contrast paper.

1) Do not write the paper in the first person (I) or refer to the second person (you).
2) The essay should consist of four paragraphs:

First paragraph (introductory paragraph):
introduce the novel and the movie
include your thesis statement
Second paragraph:
include points about the novel
Third paragraph:
include points about the movie
Fourth paragraph (concluding paragraph):
include examples of how the novel and movie are similar or different
conclude with a reworded thesis statement

3) Each paragraph must have a clear topic sentence.
4) Every sentence must support the topic sentence of that paragraph.

# *Essay Assessment I*

To help you assess your student's essay, complete the following checklist.

The essay contains:

1) a thesis statement that clearly identifies the main idea __________

2) an introductory paragraph __________

3) body paragraphs that support the main idea __________

4) a concluding paragraph __________

5) a topic sentence for each paragraph __________

6) sentences within a paragraph that relate back to the topic sentence __________

7) transitional words to relate one sentence to the next __________

8) a reworded thesis statement in the concluding paragraph __________

9) cohesiveness and unity __________

10) correct grammar, punctuation, and spelling __________

If your student has missed any of the above points, encourage him to go back and improve his essay. Congratulate him for his effort and completion.

# More Romantic Poets

1. a. Poet's Corner

**Percy Bysshe Shelley** was born in Sussex, England, on August 4, 1792. His radical and nonconformist ideas upset the moral standards of the day. While he attended the University of Oxford, he was expelled along with another student for writing and circulating *The Necessity of Atheism.* Shelley befriended William Godwin, a freethinking socialist, and soon became enamored with his young daughter, Mary Wollstonecraft Godwin. Although Shelley was married, he ran away with Mary and sailed to France, despite Mary's father's disapproval. After Shelley's wife's tragic suicide, Percy and Mary were married. Percy Shelley drowned during a storm on his way to Italy on July 8, 1822.

b. Shelley drew his philosophy from a mixture of Plato, transcendentalism, a little of Wordsworth and Coleridge, and very little from Christianity, except that he admired Christ for his love of mankind. Shelley, like Plato, believed that this world was not reality. Reality, for Shelley, was the realm of ideas, and it was his job, as a poet, to bring those ideas to the understanding of his readers. The realm of ideas was like a spiritual realm where all truth was to be transmitted through poetry. Shelley's highest ideal was love of one another. He wanted his poems to teach people to show love for one another. In this regard, he was a humanitarian, much like Wordsworth and Coleridge.

c. Read Shelley's "Hymn to Intellectual Beauty," pp. 167-169. The stanzas are like paragraphs and can be understood as units. Try to attain a grasp of each stanza as you read.

d. How would you explain (in just a sentence or two) intellectual beauty based on stanza one?

e. From reading stanza two, what does Shelley think of his present society?

f. What does Shelley's spirit of beauty do in stanza four?

g. Who are the departed dead in stanza five?

h. What shadow fell on Shelley at the end of stanza five?

i. What, above all else, does this spirit tell Shelley to do?

j. Begin writing a poem today. Choose a topic you have strong feelings about. You will have time the next two days to complete your poem.

2. a. Read Shelley's "Ode to the West Wind," pp. 169-170.

   b. At the time this poem was written, Shelley thought he was dying. He felt that his message was not being received and that time was running out for him to spread his word.

   c. Read the poem aloud.

   d. Continue working on your poem, if necessary.

3. a. Read stanza one again. Of what do you think the West Wind is symbolic?

   b. Notice that the West Wind is an Autumn wind. It drives leaves and seeds. What do the leaves and seeds represent?

   c. What natural element is being driven by the wind in stanza two? What is dispensed?

   d. Note: Baiae is an ancient Roman summer resort. What element is driven in stanza three?

   e. Shelley wishes to be a cloud, a wave, or a leaf, driven by the West Wind. Is this a good comparison? Explain.

   f. In stanza six, Shelley adds a dimension to the poem. What is it?

   g. Continue working on your poem, if necessary.

4. a. Read Shelley's "To a Skylark," stanzas one to six, beginning on page 173.

   As you read, keep in mind that the skylark sings before dawn and after dark. It can be heard, but not seen.

   b. Look up any words you don't know. You should have a fairly long list from the poem.

c. What do you think the skylark symbolizes?

5. a. Read stanzas seven to twelve of "To a Skylark," beginning on page 174. Look at the four similes (stanzas eight to eleven). What do the four similes have in common?

   b. In the next six stanzas, what do you think Shelley is saying?

   c. Consider the last three stanzas. Do you think that Shelley feels that his message will be accepted?

1.

d. It is an unseen power–a spiritual force–that surrounds us.

e. He describes our "state" as a "dim vast vale of tears, vacant and desolate."

Note: The last two lines of stanza two refer to opposites. In Shelley's frame of reference, these opposites must be reconciled, and stanza three says that only the spirit of beauty is capable of doing so.

f. It is capable of imparting love, hope, self-esteem, sympathies (in the broadest sense) and is otherwise capable of nourishing the human heart.

g. The dead are the philosophers and perhaps theologians and anyone who wrote on life's values, its meaning, etc.

h. The spirit of beauty fell on Shelley. This is Shelley's personal revelation.

i. This spirit tells him to "love all human kind" (last line of the poem).

Note: Shelley called the power behind the universe necessitating reality. This suggests that one is motivated to carry out love for mankind once one is in touch with this spirit.

3.

a. The West Wind represents the spirit behind the universe that Shelley thinks is the source of love, understanding, etc.

b. Autumn leaves are old symbols for something that doesn't have long to live. The seeds, however, represent new thoughts that will be born in the spring.

c. Clouds. They dispense rain, hail, and lightning.

d. Water. The wind drives the waves all across the Mediterranean and the Atlantic.

e. Since the West Wind represents the spiritual force that Shelley wants us to be in tune with, he has chosen natural elements that are driven by the wind. He is trying to provide a concrete picture of an abstract idea. He wants the reader to think about interacting with and being surrounded by the spiritual force.

f. Like the clouds, waves, and leaves, Shelley wishes his words would be distributed over the earth for people to absorb. Like Wordsworth and Coleridge, he wanted to touch something in people so that they would change their hearts for the better.

4.

c. The first stanza tells us that Shelley gives a spiritual quality to the skylark, as if it were a voice from the spiritual world. Stanzas two through six say much the same thing, only a little differently each time.

5.

a. They are all things, which are hidden or obscured, yet project something good beyond

**their confining circumstances. Shelley certainly refers to himself in stanza eight, and perhaps others, such as Wordsworth, Coleridge, and Keats.**

b. **Shelley suggests that the skylark, in tune with the spiritual world, must know things that we don't, and therefore communicates the things of the spirit–love, beauty, truth, etc.**

c. **There isn't much optimism in the last stanza. Shelley seems to say that the skylark projects its love and joy over a gloomy world, and that Shelley might be the only one listening. However, Shelley probably also knew that this poem, like the skylark's song, would be read and heard far beyond Shelley's own place and even beyond his own time. He probably felt somewhat satisfied that his message of love would never be completely disregarded.**

1. a. Poet's Corner

**John Keats** was born on October 31, 1795, to a livery-stable owner in London. His parents both died before he was fifteen. He did not even begin to write poetry until he was eighteen years old. Despite this inauspicious conception, his poetry has become some of the most recognizable writing from his period. He has penned such famous lines as "A thing of beauty is a joy forever" (from "Endymion") and "Beauty is truth, truth beauty" (from "Ode on a Grecian Urn"). Along with Wordsworth, he is considered the greatest writer of sonnets from the romantic period. He contracted tuberculosis and died shortly thereafter at the age of twenty-five on February 23, 1821. In his last personal letter, he wrote to his intimate friend, Charles Brown, ending, "I can scarcely bid you goodbye even in a letter. I always made an awkward bow. God bless you. John Keats."

"No one can read Keats' poems and letters without an undersense of the tragic waste of so extraordinary an intellect and genius cut off so early. What he might have accomplished is beyond conjecture; what we do know is that his achievement, when he stopped writing at the age of twenty-four, greatly exceeds that at the same age of Chaucer, Shakespeare, or Milton" (1822, Norton).

b. Read "On First Looking into Chapman's Homer" on page 191. This was Keats' first successful poem, published in 1816. George Chapman was a British translator of Homer's writings.

c. What does Keats mean by "realms of gold" and "western islands"? Keep in mind the title and purpose of the sonnet.

d. Who are the "bards" he talks about?

e. What is Apollo associated with in Roman mythology (besides the sun)?

f. Define demesne and ken.

g. In a few sentences, describe in your own words how Keats

felt upon first reading Chapman's Homer. Why does he compare it to the things he does?

h. Begin writing poetry today. Remember to show your readers, not tell. Avoid the abstract; be clear and concrete. You will have two days to complete your poem.

2. a. Read Keats' "When I Have Fears that I May Cease to Be" on page 192.

   b. What type of sonnet is this—Shakespearean or Petrarchan/ Classical? (Refer to Lessons 2 and 6.)

   c. What does the poet fear? Why is this poem especially poignant for Keats?

   d. What is the "full-ripened grain"?

   e. Continue working on your poem, if necessary.

3. a. John Keats' central idea was to create beauty through his poetry that would last indefinitely. This common theme in the arts views the work of art as something eternal, everlasting. The work of art, then, achieves immortality for the artist. Although the artist dies, he lives on through the works that are left. The sad fact that the artist lives in time and must fade in terms of his own youth and beauty was a condition that Keats called melancholy. Although there is melancholy in the fact that the artist's youth and beauty must fade, there is joy in the knowledge that beauty in his works of art remain to give him immortality.

   b. Read Keats' "A Thing of Beauty," on page 201. Note: The excerpt, "A Thing of Beauty," is from "Endymion."

   Keats' early attempt at achieving an immortal poem is a lengthy work entitled "Endymion." The first line, "A thing of beauty is a joy forever," is often quoted. Unfortunately, little else about the poem is memorable, and the critics of Keats' day were quick to condemn it. Stunned, but not devastated, Keats pondered his critics' observations and learned from his mistakes. His subsequent poetry achieved the status he had hoped for and places him as one of England's greatest poets.

c. How would you summarize the meaning of the first thirteen lines?

d. What is Keats trying to do in lines 13-24?

e. Why did Keats' critics say that his poem was poorly written and failed to reach its artistic goal?

f. Continue working on your poem, if necessary.

4. a. Read Keats' "Ode on Melancholy," page 193.

The references to Greek mythology can be found in the dictionary. If you don't know these allusions, be sure to look them up so you can understand the full content of the poem.

b. Summarize the meaning of the first stanza.

c. In stanza two, what remedies are suggested to resist melancholy?

d. How does stanza three summarize the meaning of the poem?

5. a. Read John Keats' "Ode on a Grecian Urn," pp. 196-197.

Note that the urn of this poem is an imaginary one. Keats is creating out of the power of his imagination—something that does not fade or change over time.

b. What is Keats' mind in the process of doing in stanza one?

c. How do you interpret stanza two?

d. What additional timeless element is added to beauty in stanza three?

e. In stanza five, what does Keats mean by "When old age shall this generation waste, Thou shalt remain."

1.
c. He is referring to books.

d. Bards are the writers.

e. He is also associated with music, poetry, and healing.

f. demesne - one's domain
ken - one's field of vision

g. Answers will vary.

2.
b. It is a Shakespearean sonnet. Note the rhyme scheme.

c. The poet fears that he will die before he has fully expressed in writing all that his mind holds. More than this, he also despairs at the prospect of losing his "fair creature of an hour."

These were very real emotions and situations for Keats. He probably anticipated an early death and produced an unparalleled collection of poetry in such a short amount of time.

d. It is the culmination of his thoughts and emotions expressed on paper.

3.
c. Keats opens by saying that beauty (a work of art) is a source of everlasting pleasure. He says that it will keep us from being overwhelmed by worldly concerns. Lines 4 and 5 suggest that pleasure is our escape from reality.

d. He is trying to create beauty through a series of images. The purpose is to absorb the reader and allow him to escape into the beauty of the poem.

e. Notice that the poem tells us what to think rather than show us. Keats' opening lines are prosaic, even a little didactic. Rather than leading the reader, Keats preaches to him. A good poem shows its intent and allows the reader to use his imagination to arrive at the meaning.

4.
b. Keats says to resist the tendency to flee from life's responsibilities. Notice that this is a contrast to "Endymion," in which he advocates escapism.

c. Keats advises us to fill ourselves with beauty–"a morning rose," "globed peonies,"–and love. These things are eternal and don't die. Notice that Keats shows us the remedy rather than trying to provide us the remedy as he does in"Endymion." Keats laid out the images for us. In "Ode on Melancholy," he directs us to go see for ourselves. He shows us the way.

d. Keats reminds us that a person's youth and beauty must pass away. Therefore, we must retain beauty in our imagination where it never fades. If we don't do this, then melancholy will eventually wear us down and claim us "among her cloudy trophies."

5.
b. He is observing the urn. He turns it around in his mind

and observes the paintings on it. His questions show that he is pondering what the urn means to him.

c. Keats pictures this scene in his mind, as if it were a painting on an urn. The last two lines remind us that paintings on urns survive over time.

d. Love is added.

e. Keats reminds us that people grow old and die. However, a work of art, which is created by the imagination, survives. Since the urn of this poem is imaginary in the first place, Keats is showing us that the reviving power of beauty can be at hand by using one's imagination. In this case, Keats' example is an urn of his own creation which was stimulated by his memories of Grecian urns he has seen.

# Emma

**Teacher's Note: The beginning of this lesson includes a summary of the novel. This is designed to help you discuss the novel with the student. Also, some students are better able to understand the novel if they read a summary; however, it should not replace reading the full novel. Please note that any surprise element or suspense is revealed in the summary. Use the summary to best meet your student's needs.**

Lessons 15-19 Novel Unit - *Emma* by Jane Austen
Published by Bantam Books ISBN 0-553-21273-7

Note: Perhaps some of the male readers will be rather distressed when they learn that they will be studying Jane Austen this school year. Unfortunately, many people unthinkingly consider Austen a writer solely for women. In *Emma*, the main character is a young woman; women carry a majority of the dialogue; and, sadly for some perhaps, there is no physical violence. However, those who are disappointed by the former will be at least as pleased upon learning that, in the novel (and in all of Austen's other novels), there are no improbable, long-winded, indulgent professions of love and they contain much satirical wit and humor.

1. a. Link to the Author: Jane Austen

Before moving into the Victorian period, we must travel back three decades to the turn of the century and the beginning of the romantic period. The period produced only two significant novelists—Sir Walter Scott and Jane Austen. Austen was born on December 16, 1775, in Steventon, England. Ignoring the literary circles of her time, she quietly crept onto the literary stage, bringing forth a distinguished collection of novels in a remarkably short period of time. During her lifetime, she wrote six major novels: *Sense and Sensibility* (1811), *Pride and Prejudice* (1813), *Mansfield Park* (1814), and *Emma* (1816); including two novels which were published posthumously: *Northanger Abbey* (1818) and *Persuasion* (1818). Although she was a favorite of her contemporary, Scott, Austen was not nearly as well accepted as Scott in her time. She died at the age of forty-one. She has rapidly gained popularity and, today, is one of the most well-known writers from the period.

Jane Austen is not so easy to categorize and define as are writers such as William Wordsworth or John Keats. She can only be defined as transitional, which, as we know, is a poor enough definition after all. Although she falls within the general boundaries of the romantic period (1780-1840)—she was born in 1775—Austen cannot be compared with the

the other writers in the romantic period. Her novels address none of the romantic ideologies regarding nature or the imagination, and she shows no interest in addressing the various revolutions of the time—in politics and in thought and artistic theory. At the same time, while she writes of real things and real people (i.e., her characters do not take on the lordly mannerisms and difficult prose of characters from the neoclassicists before her), her prose was also more real, less flowery than those writers before her. Many critics feel that her greatest asset in writing was simply that she wrote of what she knew. Because of her importance as a writer in this period of British literature and as a major influence on later writers, especially in the craft and form of the novel, we would be sorely amiss to exclude her.

b. Summary of *Emma*

Emma Woodhouse is an attractive, wealthy twenty-one year old who lives dutifully with her widower father in Highbury. Emma, believing that she brought about the marriage of Anne Taylor, her governess and friend of many years, to Mr. Weston, now plans on uniting Mr. Elton with Harriet Smith. Harriet is in love with Robert Martin, but Emma insists that she must not marry a farmer, and convinces Harriet to marry "above herself." George Knightley, her brother-in-law, disagrees with Emma's antics and speaks highly of Robert as a good man. Emma's attempt backfires when she discovers that Mr. Elton is in love with her (Emma).

Mr. and Mrs. Weston do a little matchmaking themselves with Frank Churchill and Emma. Frank (Mr. Weston's son from a former marriage) is a proper and handsome man, and Emma is convinced that he is in love with her. Her error is discovered when it is later revealed that Frank and Jane Fairfax had been secretly engaged. As the story continues, Harriet tells Emma about her new love for someone "above her." All along, Emma assumes that Harriet is in love with Frank Churchill. Emma is not only surprised when Harriet reveals the man as George Knightley, but immediately acknowledges her own feelings towards him. The big muddle created by Emma is undone and everyone is married into their own social rank. Harriet marries her original suitor, Robert Martin; and Emma marries George Knightley, "just as it should be."

c. Major characters in Emma:

Emma Woodhouse (Hartfield): twenty-one year old attractive daughter of her widower father
Henry Woodhouse (Hartfield): Emma's father
George Knightley (Donwell Abbey): Emma's brother-in-law, a long time friend
John and Isabella Knightley (Brunswick Square, London): George's brother and Emma's sister respectively
Mr. and Mrs. Weston (Randalls): the Woodhouses' neighbor
Frank Churchill (Enscombe): Mr. Weston's son by a former marriage
Harriet Smith (Mrs. Goddard's house): seventeen-year-old whom Emma tries to marry off
Miss Bates: an old maid
Jane Fairfax (with the Campbells, then with the Bateses): Miss Bates' niece
Mr. Elton (vicarage of Highbury): the rector whom Emma tries to match up with Harriet

d. Note: It is extremely important in reading Austen's novels to understand the ideals and prejudices of the time. A complete understanding of terms like *class* and *identity* is necessary. In today's society, class is usually determined by economic prosperity. Eighteenth century England had very defined, very rigid social distinctions. Class is one's social rank or position. While one's holdings, monetary or other, and one's education are also factors, we shall find that these are largely not as important as the position of one's parents.

The narration in *Emma* is very straightforward and easy to follow. The prose itself is not extremely complicated and is certainly within the scope of high school readers. There are a fairly high number of characters as well as a number of residences to keep up with, so refer to the brief list of characters in **1c** as needed.

However, there are some themes throughout the novel that some younger readers may not notice on their own. For example, some young readers may not expect to find a writer poking fun at her own heroine (as Austen often does to Emma). Emma, in fact, has many faults (many excellent qualities as well!), and it is important for the student to recognize that Austen criticizes heroines and antagonists alike, each according to their faults. There are no perfect characters. Austen said of Emma Woodhouse, "I am going to make a heroine whom no one but myself will much like." I think you will find that Austen proved incorrect of her assessment of Emma.

To answer many of the questions in this unit, one must pay close attention to the personality and disposition of the characters. Austen's novels depend especially on the depth and fullness of her characters. With her characters, readers quickly learn their mannerisms and habits. Her major characters are so realistic and defined, that, just like you and me, they sometimes even slip out-of-character.

e. Read Chapters 1-2.

f. Chapter 1
Upon the evolution of Miss Taylor into Mrs. Weston, both Mr. Woodhouse and Emma feel some amount of sorrow. Describe Mr. Woodhouse's and Emma's feelings.

g. How is Mr. Knightley unique in his relationship with Emma?

h. Chapter 2
What does the section of narrative regarding Frank Churchill's letter to his father tell the reader of the village of Highbury and its inhabitants?

2. a. Read Chapters 3-4.

b. Chapter 3
Describe Miss Bates' situation in life. What does this tell you about the social standings and divisions of the time?

c. Describe Miss Harriet Smith.

d. Chapter 4
Why does Emma befriend Harriet? What is her reasoning?

e. Why does Emma try to persuade Harriet to forget about Mr. Martin?

3. a. Read Chapters 5-6.

b. How does Mr. Knightley regard Emma differently from Mrs. Weston?

c. Mr. Knightley says that Emma has little to gain from the relationship with Harriet, but why does he also feel that Harriet will not improve herself in her companionship with Emma?

d. Chapter 6
What is Mr. Elton's social class? Although Emma says (in Ch. 4) that a match between Harriet and Mr. Elton "was what everyone else must think of and predict" (p. 31), what are your thoughts on the match?

e. What does Mr. Elton seem to admire more—the portrait or the model?

4. a. Read Chapters 7-9.

b. Chapter 7
Describe the interactions between Emma and Harriet regarding Mr. Martin's letter. What character traits are revealed?

c. Chapter 8
When Mr. Knightley expresses his dismay and disapproval of Harriet's refusal of Mr. Martin, Emma replies, "Oh, to be sure, it is always incomprehensible to a man, that a woman should ever refuse an offer of marriage. A man always imagines a woman to be ready for anybody who asks her" (p. 55). What is the significance of this statement?

d. We know why Emma thinks Harriet deserves better than Mr. Martin. Why does Mr. Knightley see things exactly opposite?

e. How do Emma and Mr. Knightley differ in their confidences (after they leave each other, following their argument)?

f. Mr. Knightley says that Mr. Elton is looking elsewhere for a wife. Why does this not deter Emma's designs for both Mr. Elton and her friend, Harriet?

g. Chapter 9
While Emma has succeeded in bringing Harriet into higher society as she originally intended, she has not succeeded in some of her other ventures with Harriet. What has she failed to do with Harriet that she had previously intended, and what does this say about Emma?

h. Why do you think Mr. Elton seems so confused when Emma thanks him for "his friend's" charade?

5. As we have seen, Emma exhibits an air of conceit along with her considerable charm. How does Austen get away with writing about a heroine so wrapped up in herself? Write two to three paragraphs describing your assessment of Emma's character. Explain what it is about Emma that is so endearing. Include many examples from the story describing Emma's good and bad qualities.

1.

f. Mr. Woodhouse grieves over the loss of "poor Miss Taylor" chiefly because he believes that she was much better off as the governess of the house at Hartfield than as the lady of her own household at Randalls. He is very close-minded (in a charmingly naive sort of way), and, as he himself could not bear such a drastic change in lifestyle, he cannot very well understand how she could bear it any other way either.

   For Emma, Miss Taylor had long ceased to be her governess and had taken on the role of friend and sisterly companion. While she is honestly delighted for her friend, she is sorry that their friendship should be inevitably changed.

g. He is "one of the few people who could see faults in Emma Woodhouse, and the only one who ever told her of them" (p. 8).

h. Everyone in the village seems to have an opinion on the matter, a positive one, and the letter, its addresser, and its addressee are the subject of much talk and conjecture about the sleepy, gossipy, little village.

2.

b. Miss Bates is not young, attractive, well to do, or married. Neither is she educated or particularly intelligent or witty. She is presently bound to her elderly, dependent mother. Because she has no money and she has not married into any high social position, she will probably live out her life in her present social condition, or even drop lower than she is now. However, she bears it all remarkably well and is well known about Highbury as a happy, benevolent woman.

   The character of Miss Bates brings into light the subject of class. Class is one's social rank or position. In today's society, class is usually determined by economic prosperity. In *Emma*, we shall find that, in general, one's family or lineage determines one's class. We shall discuss this topic further throughout the novel.

c. She is remarkably beautiful, which piques Emma's interest in her. However, she does not seem to be particularly clever, and she gives away her class by unaffectedly displaying her awe of the elegance of Hartfield. She is very complaisant and acquiescent towards Emma, and she is extremely charming. Physically, she is short and "plump," with light hair and soft blue eyes. Emma determines that she "should not be wasted on the inferior society of Highbury and its connections" (p. 20). For her part, Miss Smith (or Harriet as she shall be referred to subsequently) is delighted that the famous and high-standing Miss Woodhouse should take interest in her.

d. Emma desires a new friend to replace Mrs. Weston, but she looks at Harriet more as a commodity that will be useful to her. Emma feels that she (Emma) will be useful to

Harriet. "For Mrs. Weston there was nothing to be done; for Harriet everything" (p. 23)—Harriet is Emma's "project."

e. Emma sees that Mr. Martin is no gentleman, and she does not want her friend to have anything to do with a simple farmer. Emma herself would never condescend to befriend anyone who she believes is below her class. Also, Emma believes that Harriet is higher-born than the Martins, despite her questionable parentage. (Recall the importance of family with regards to class.) In those respects, she is looking out for Harriet as well as herself.

3.

b. He sees that Emma has the misfortune of being the most intelligent person in her family ever since she was very young. She has always been more clever than her sister, Isabella, who is seven years older. Also she has run the household since she was twelve, when her mother died. Mr. Knightley feels that she has not had the benefit of being very often corrected or even shown to be wrong. (Note: Austen uses this discussion between Mrs. Weston and Mr. Knightley to tell the reader about Emma's history and physical appearance.)

c. He says that Harriet will only become smug in her newfound position among Highbury's elite. She will learn just enough from Emma to make her unhappy in her own surroundings.

d. Mr. Elton, a recent addition to Highbury, is the preacher (he married Mr. and Mrs. Weston) and is a gentleman, being "without low connections" (p. 31). His social class is also determined by the fact that he is known to be in the possession of some independent property. Because of the difference in their social standings, a match between Harriet and Mr. Elton seems highly dubious at this point. But we shall see.

e. He certainly gives more praise to Miss Woodhouse's likeness (portrait).

4.

b. Harriet is entirely unable to make a decision for herself. She has come to depend completely on the judgment of her friend. Note how Emma controls Harriet with the mere inflection of her voice. She feigns surprise and embarrassment at having "misunderstood" Harriet's original intent (Harriet certainly would have accepted if not for Emma), and Harriet soon realizes how far beneath her Mr. Martin really is. Harriet can be very dependent and naive; Emma can be very controlling—together, they suit each other quite well, although, as Mr. Knightley warns, their intimacy is "a bad thing" (p. 32) for both.

Emma seems to feel that Harriet is a child who must be guided, prodded, even disciplined in order to move her in the right direction. Emma's comment that she would not, could not visit Harriet at Abbey-

Mill Farm is quite vicious and tells us much of Emma's thoughts regarding the social caste system of the day.

Note also the humor in the chapter; Harriet often serves as the comic relief in the novel. Harriet says, "Miss Woodhouse, as you will not give me your opinion, I must do as well as I can by myself; and I have now quite determined, and really almost made up my mind, to refuse Mr. Martin. Do you think I am right?" (p. 48). Emma, of course, has just previously instructed Harriet on how to decline Mr. Martin's proposal. Did you also pick up on Emma referring to Harriet informally, while Harriet still calls Emma by the more formal, unfamiliar "Miss Woodhouse"?

c. Austen is striking a note for the independence of women.

d. To him, Harriet has no high claims to parentage, money, or education. He sees Mr. Martin as a "respectable, intelligent, gentleman-farmer" (p. 57). (It is doubtful that Emma would ever use "gentleman" and "farmer" like this.) Mr. Knightley saw the attachment as much to the benefit of Harriet. He also suspects Emma of interfering with Harriet's affections. With fairness to all, Mr. Knightley knows little of Harriet and probably does not give her the credit she deserves. And because of her social prejudices, Emma certainly does not give credit to Mr. Martin at all.

e. As the omniscient narrator tells us, Mr. Knightley is always very confident in his opinions, while Emma is not as self-assured of her correctness as is Mr. Knightley.

f. Emma is very confident in herself, because she believes that Mr. Elton showed great interest in Harriet when Emma was painting her likeness. Emma has put much stock in her understanding of Mr. Elton's affections.

g. Emma wanted to educate her and "improve Harriet's mind," but each book that they started was soon forgotten. Emma, it seems, has a history of not finishing what she begins—many of her paintings are only half-finished.

h. He clearly expected Emma to say more about the riddle than she did. What he expected, I leave up to you.

1. a. Read Chapters 10-12 of Jane Austen's *Emma*.

   b. Chapter 10
   Why does Emma not want to marry?

   c. Who is Jane Fairfax, and why does Emma dislike her?

   d. Chapter 11
   Why does Emma not get along particularly well with Mr. Knightley's younger brother, Mr. John Knightley?

   e. Chapter 12
   Why doesn't Mr. Woodhouse wish Mr. Knightley to join the family for dinner?

   f. How did Mr. Martin take the news of Harriet's refusal?

   g. In what humorous way are Mr. Woodhouse and his eldest daughter similar in their eating habits, and different from all others present?

   h. Under what circumstances does a disagreement arise between Mr. John Knightley and Mr. Woodhouse?

2. a. Read Chapters 13-15.

   b. Chapter 13
   Surprisingly, Mr. Woodhouse decides to venture from his safe haven at Hartfield to attend the Christmas party at Randalls. What persuaded him to go?

   c. Who else is invited to the party?

   d. What does Mr. Elton say when he learns of Harriet's illness?

   e. What does Mr. John Knightley think about Mr. Elton's love life?

   f. How are Mr. Elton's and Mr. John Knightley's tastes regarding socializing different?

g. Chapter 14
As Mr. Elton becomes more and more friendly towards Emma, what does she begin to think?

h. How does Emma feel about Mr. Frank Churchill?

i. Why is a promise from Frank Churchill to visit no guarantee at all?

j. Chapter 15
What do Mr. John Knightley, Mr. Weston, and Mr. Knightley say about the snowfall that evening? How does this illustrate the differences in their character?

k. How does Jane Austen describe Mr. Elton's actions towards Emma in the coach?

l. What does Mr. Elton think about Emma's hopes that he was in love with Harriet? Use our definition of class in your answer.

3. a. Read Chapters 16-18

b. Chapter 16
Why is Emma doubly saddened by this unseen turn of events?

c. How has Mr. Elton's character changed in Emma's mind?

d. Do you think that Mr. Elton's only reason for seeking Emma was monetary? Explain your answer.

e. Emma begins to think of how inferior Mr. Elton is to her. This gives us a chance to further explore our definition of social class. How do the social positions of Mr. Woodhouse/ Emma (the heiress), Mr. Knightley and Mr. Elton measure against each other?

f. How does Emma now feel about her matchmaking?

g. Chapter 17
Why is Mr. Woodhouse not surprised by the omission of Emma from Mr. Elton's departure letter?

h. How does Harriet feel about Emma when she learns that Mr. Elton does not reciprocate Harriet's affections?

i. Chapter 18
What does Mr. Knightley think about Mr. Frank Churchill's "letter of excuse"?

j. What does Emma say about Mr. Knightley's accusations?

k. What does Mr. Knightley's reply to this tell you about his character?

4. a. Read Chapters 19-21.

b. Chapter 19
How is Emma often remiss in her neighborly duties when it comes to Mrs. and Miss Bates? Why is she negligent?

c. What is Emma's greatest fear in visiting the Bateses?

d. Chapter 20
Describe the upbringing of Jane Fairfax. How was her class improved?

e. Why do you think Emma dislikes Jane Fairfax?

f. Emma decides to try to be friendlier to Jane. But what about Jane makes this difficult for Emma?

g. Chapter 21
What juicy bit of news arrives at Hartfield in this chapter?

h. After Miss Bates and her niece leave Hartfield, what is Emma's immediate concern?

i. How do Elizabeth Martin and Robert Martin react to seeing Harriet for the first time since she turned down Robert's proposal?

j. Why is Emma troubled by their kind manners?

k. Emma tells Harriet that she "behaved extremely well" (p.163). Do you see this from Harriet's telling of the events?

5. You have now been given a chance to observe extensively the rigorous mandates of interclass social behavior in the early nineteenth century. What do you think of it? How is behavior toward those outside of one's social class in the story's time period different from behavior toward those outside of one's social class today? How is it similar? Write a few paragraphs comparing and contrasting the two.

1.

b. She says, if married, "I cannot really change for the better" (p. 78). However, this must not be taken for conceit (recall from Ch. 5, that Mr. Knightley, who, of all people, would find fault in Emma, does not think her vain at all), rather as satisfaction with her present position in life. She doesn't need anything, and she doesn't want anything that she does not have. She admits that, were she to fall in love, things would surely be different, but she sees no prospects presently.

c. She is the niece of Miss Bates (we shall learn more about her parentage later), which, for Emma, is one strike against her, for Emma has little patience for Miss Bates' endless prattle. And so, Jane Fairfax has become repulsive to Emma by association.

d. Mr. John Knightley (as he is called, to avoid confusion with George Knightley) has an impatient temper, and since Isabella is so deferential to him, he is sometimes harsh or short with her—Emma is more offended than Isabella. Also, like his brother, Mr. John Knightley is not so quick to praise her as some others in Highbury. Mostly though, she dislikes his lack of complete indulgence and tolerance of her father's ways.

e. Mr. Woodhouse wishes to have his "poor Isabella" all to himself.

f. Mr. Knightley reports that Mr. Martin is very dejected.

g. They are both health conscious, especially Mr. Woodhouse, comedically so, and they both believe that "a nice basin of gruel" is just the thing for one's well being.

h. Isabella and her family had gone to Southend the past autumn, much to the dismay of Mr. Woodhouse at the time (and at present). He had understood from his physician, Mr. Perry, that Southend was not an agreeable place for one's physical well being. (In reality, Mr. Woodhouse had unconsciously been displacing his own beliefs onto Mr. Perry.) Mr. Woodhouse unthinkingly blunders on about their poor choice of venues, until Mr. John Knightley, fed up with his judgment being aspersed, speaks rather harshly to Mr. Woodhouse. Mr. Knightley quickly intervenes, and the conversation turns, but this is the type of situation that greatly displeases Emma regarding her brother-in-law.

2.

b. He would rather attend than to leave his dear Isabella.

c. Besides Emma, her father and the Knightley family, the others who were invited were Mr. Knightley, Mr. Elton, and Harriet.

d. He seems genuinely worried for Harriet's well-being, as well as worried about Emma's attending to her. He quickly suggests that

Mr. Perry be called. His concern perhaps is more that Emma may contract the malady than that Harriet should receive professional care.

e. He believes that Mr. Elton has affections for Emma instead of for Harriet. In her highly informed mind, Emma finds this ridiculous and amusing.

f. Mr. Elton, who is rather younger than the other, cannot get enough of parties and other social engagements. Mr. John Knightley, who is older and married, is much more sedate and conscious of moderation and sensibility.

g. She wonders if her brother-in-law was correct. However, she thinks that Mr. Elton is "beginning to transfer his affections" (p. 109) from Harriet to herself. We shall soon learn that it is somewhat more serious than that. At any rate, Mr. Elton's contrivances serve only to make her rather cross with him.

h. Although she has never met him, she enjoys imagining the possibility of her marrying him. Because of his relation to Mr. and Mrs. Weston, it seems to her to be the proper thing; after all, "he seemed, by this connection between the families, to quite belong to her" (p. 110). She is very excited about meeting him.

i. As Mrs. Weston points out, "It depends entirely upon his aunt's spirits and pleasure; in short, upon her temper" (p. 112). Mrs. Churchill is the wife of Mr. Weston's (deceased) former wife's brother. She is apparently very authoritarian and may not allow Frank to visit his father at the specified time.

j. Mr. John Knightley announced the snow suddenly and almost as if he rather enjoyed seeing the worry appear on Mr. Woodhouse's face. He continues on, saying he admires Mr. Woodhouse's bravery in coming out on such a night, and saying that if one coach does happen to overturn in the storm, the other will be along to help out the poor passengers of the first. This, of course, is all terrifying to poor Mr. Woodhouse. Mr. John Knightley can be quite inconsiderate at times.

Mr. Weston, on the other hand, claims to have known about the snow, but to have not said anything for fear of unnecessarily worrying Mr. Woodhouse. He believes that there is no danger at all, but wishes there was more snow so that the party might last longer and that everyone might stay the night at Randalls. Mr. Weston always enjoys a party, almost to too great an extent.

Mr. Knightley immediately went outside to check after his brother's report. He finds that there is hardly enough snow to cover the ground and that the clouds are clearing. He is a very sensible man and often prone to action, wishing to discover the truth for himself.

k. She does not use dialogue; she plainly describes what Mr. Elton says, and briefly describes the physical aspect of it thusly—"her hand seized, her attention demanded, and Mr. Elton actually making violent love to her [verbally, not physically]" (p. 119). Austen generally avoided passionate speeches and/or actions in her novels. In this way, she departed from many of the novels of her time.

l. Mr. Elton clearly had never once considered Harriet as a possible wife. He only saw her as a way to get closer to Emma. As he said, "Everyone has their level" (p. 122). Mr. Knightley was correct when he told Emma that Mr. Elton was sensible when it came to marriage, and that he would never marry beneath him.

3.

b. She is sorry for Harriet and just as sorry that she had been the sole cause for Harriet's infatuation with Mr. Elton.

c. She now thinks him to be "proud, assuming, conceited; very full of his own claims, and little concerned about the feelings of others" (p. 124). She believes that Mr. Elton only desired her because of her wealth and class.

d. Answers will vary.

e. Mr. Elton has no family background in Highbury that anyone knows of. Also, he has much less money/holdings than she will inherit. The Woodhouse family has been known to Hartfield for several generations and come from a still older family line. While Hartfield is not a large estate, much of her family's capital is from "other sources." Mr. Knightley's fortune is in property—nearly all of Highbury belongs to Mr. Knightley. While he does not have as much money as the Woodhouses, he is worth more. Thus, Mr. Elton is considerably below both Emma and Mr. Knightley as far as class is concerned.

f. She recognizes the problems that it can cause (and that it has caused), and she resolves to discontinue her little practice.

g. He is too concerned about Mr. Elton's health.

h. Poor, self-effacing Harriet only loves Emma the more, believing that only a true friend like Emma could ever have thought that she was good enough for a gentleman of the caliber of Mr. Elton.

i. He disapproves. He believes that a man of Frank Churchill's age and position would be able to take leave of his aunt and uncle to visit his father and his new wife more easily than it seems. He thinks that the selfishness of Mrs. Churchill has been bred into Frank Churchill as well.

j. He should not make such indictments without proof and without knowledge of his family situation.

k. Mr. Knightley stresses a man's duty to his family. He also stresses the importance of straightforward decisions and action. Mr. Knightley is very strongly opinionated (as we have seen) and values genuineness and emotional strength. Emma, however, reminds Mr. Knightley that Frank Churchill is still dependent on his aunt and uncle, and that such strong statements to one's guardians would be impolite. In fact, Mr. Knightley's inclination to dislike Frank Churchill is somewhat out of character for him. However, the entire conversation between Emma and Mr. Knightley defines their respective characters very well.

4.

b. Mr. Knightley has often told her that she is not as kind as she should be nor as generous with her time and money towards the Bateses. They live in rather humble conditions, especially as compared to Hartfield.

She declines to visit with them mainly for two reasons: Miss Bates is extremely long-winded, and secondly, as Emma sees it, their guests consist of the second and third rate citizens of Highbury, and Emma would not deign to be grouped with such as these.

c. Emma fears that she might be read letters from Jane Fairfax. Miss Bates is extremely proud of her niece and will compliment her on anything. As a result, complimenting Jane is sure to win the sincerest gratitude of Miss Bates.

d. Jane was born in Highbury, and at three years of age, both parents died, so she lived with her grandmother and aunt. A military friend of her father's, Col. Campbell offered to bring her up, and as he was in a much better position to do this well, he was allowed. She went to live with the Colonel's family, which included a daughter about her age, at the age of nine. Thus, she received an education that would help her to attain a higher class than would have been afforded her had she stayed with her grandmother and aunt.

e. Emma is not quite sure of that herself, although Mr. Knightley believes that she is somewhat jealous of Jane's accomplishments and reputation in Highbury. Perhaps also, since she was always expected to have been friends with Jane, she rebelled against it entirely. You may agree or have other opinions.

f. Jane is very polite, to the extent of not ever saying anything of substance. Naturally, Emma dislikes her reservedness.

g. Mr. Elton is to be married to a Miss Hawkins, even though he has only been away from Highbury for four weeks.

h. Emma is afraid that Miss Bates and her niece shall meet Harriet, who is coming to Hartfield, and tell her of Mr. Elton's engagement.

i. Elizabeth is determined to be polite and kind and greets

Harriet, although not as congenially as before. Robert also greets her (we know from Mr. Knightley how devastated he was by her refusal), and, anticipating that she will be going to Hartfield, he suggests a safe, alternate route, as the rain has washed out her normal path. As Emma sees it, "there had been an interesting mixture of wounded affection and genuine delicacy in their behavior" (p. 163).

j. Emma is faced with two differing opinions of the Martins. On one hand, she feels that they are far below her socially and that to fraternize with them would be socially unacceptable and embarrassing. On the other, she sees how forthright and noble (both qualities of gentlemen and gentlewomen) they were to Harriet, despite her unkindness to them. She solves her cognitive dissonance by deciding that they only hoped to befriend Harriet as a means to higher themselves socially.

k. Actually, the Martins behaved much better than did Harriet. Harriet noticed them just as they noticed her, but she failed to greet them. Simple gentility, a necessary quality of higher social class, demanded that she at least acknowledge them, but they were the ones to greet her instead. If Emma were in Harriet's situation, she would certainly have performed more admirably (her upbringing would have made this almost instinctive), even if she were as embarrassed as Harriet was. Harriet obviously did not have the excellent breeding that Emma had. Hopefully, we are beginning to suspect that one's mannerisms play a larger role in one's class than Emma believes.

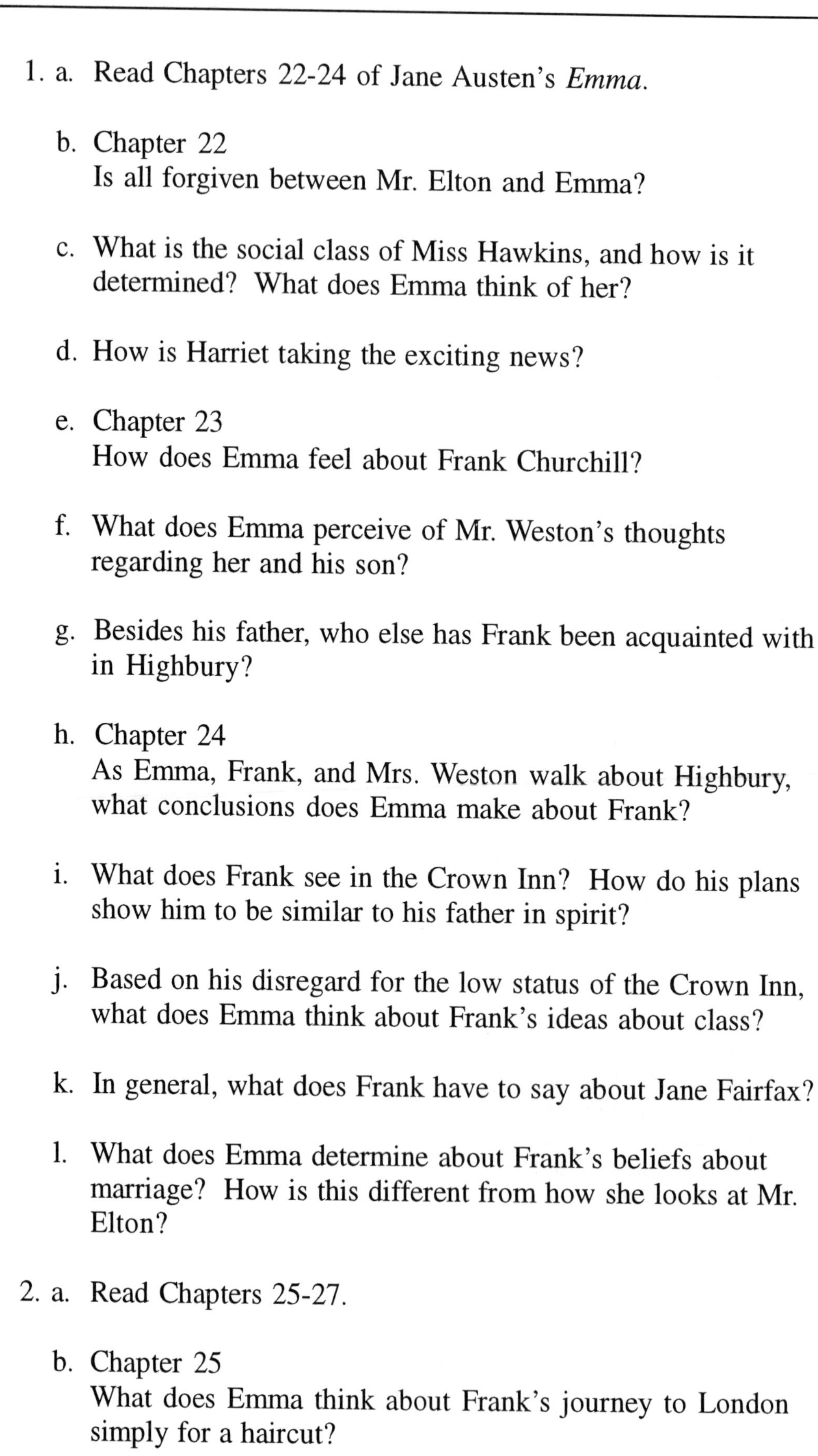

1. a. Read Chapters 22-24 of Jane Austen's *Emma*.

   b. Chapter 22
   Is all forgiven between Mr. Elton and Emma?

   c. What is the social class of Miss Hawkins, and how is it determined? What does Emma think of her?

   d. How is Harriet taking the exciting news?

   e. Chapter 23
   How does Emma feel about Frank Churchill?

   f. What does Emma perceive of Mr. Weston's thoughts regarding her and his son?

   g. Besides his father, who else has Frank been acquainted with in Highbury?

   h. Chapter 24
   As Emma, Frank, and Mrs. Weston walk about Highbury, what conclusions does Emma make about Frank?

   i. What does Frank see in the Crown Inn? How do his plans show him to be similar to his father in spirit?

   j. Based on his disregard for the low status of the Crown Inn, what does Emma think about Frank's ideas about class?

   k. In general, what does Frank have to say about Jane Fairfax?

   l. What does Emma determine about Frank's beliefs about marriage? How is this different from how she looks at Mr. Elton?

2. a. Read Chapters 25-27.

   b. Chapter 25
   What does Emma think about Frank's journey to London simply for a haircut?

   c. Describe the Coles in terms of their class.

d. What factors convince Emma to accept the Coles' invitation?

e. Chapter 26
How are class boundaries displayed at the Coles' dinner?

f. What gift did Jane receive? Who do they guess sent it?

g. Who does Emma think sent the piano? Why does she suspect this?

h. What match does Mrs. Weston propose? Who does she think is the mysterious benefactor of Jane?

i. Chapter 27
In this chapter, we learn quite a bit about perhaps the two silliest characters in the novel, although they are both quite likable. Describe the actions of Harriet and Miss Bates and how they reflect their personalities.

3. a. Read Chapters 28-30.

b. Chapter 28
How does Frank act towards Jane while they are at the Bates'?

c. How does Mr. Knightley deal with Miss Bates and her talkative ways?

d. Chapter 29
What plans for dancing does Frank have on his mind? What input do the others give?

e. When Frank's father suggests that Frank fetch two women from the Bates' residence to the Inn for their opinions, Frank wonders at the idea of the elderly Mrs. Bates being asked for her opinion. Mr. Weston obviously meant Jane instead. Why do you think that Frank does not even think of Jane and that he is somewhat rude to her at times?

f. Chapter 30
What does Mr. Knightley think about the plans? And Jane Fairfax?

g. Why must Frank suddenly leave Highbury?

h. What does Emma think is the reason for Frank's awkward, unfinished conversation at Hartfield? Do you agree?

4. a. Read Chapters 31-33.

b. Chapter 31
Why does Emma decide that she is not very much in love? What does she think about Frank's affections for her?

c. Now that Mr. Elton's impending marriage is the talk of the town, Harriet is once more depressed. What new tactic does Emma employ to try to get Harriet to cheer up?

d. Chapter 32
How does Harriet feel after she and Emma visit Mr. and Mrs. Elton?

e. What does Emma dislike about Mrs. Elton, particularly about her manners?

f. What does Mrs. Elton compare Hartfield to? Why?

g. What does Mrs. Elton say about Mrs. Weston?

h. Chapter 33
How do Mr. and Mrs. Elton use Harriet to attack Emma?

i. To whom has Mrs. Elton taken an especial liking? What about this relationship confuses Emma?

j. How does Mr. Knightley react when Emma asks him about his affections for Jane?

k. What does Mr. Knightley say about Jane's character?

l. What does Mrs. Weston say to Emma after Mr. Knightley has left them?

5. It seems that Emma prides herself on being an excellent judge of character, as the sheer quantity of her opinions of

others might suggest. But how is her judgment often clouded, particularly with regard to Harriet and Jane? Why might she be, at times, mistaken in her opinions regarding them? Write two to three paragraphs defending your position in your assessment of the two young women.

1.

b. Despite Emma's expressed happiness for Mr. Elton, he is still wounded by the conversation in the coach and is not particularly pleasant towards her.

c. Miss Hawkins brings with her at least 10,000 pounds, but her family name is of little consequence in Hartfield. Her father is a merchant in Bristol (both parents have passed away). Her main claim is that her older sister is married to a very wealthy gentleman "who kept two carriages" (p. 167). Because of this connection and because of her fortune, she must be considered to be fairly high class, especially for Hartfield, although somewhat lower than Mr. Knightley or the Woodhouses.

   Emma feels that Miss Hawkins' parentage must be lower than others thought and that her good connection to the rich brother-in-law is too far a relation to be of much importance. To Emma, "it did not appear that she was at all Harriet's superior" (p. 166).

d. Harriet is still completely infatuated with Mr. Elton. She thinks of nothing else. It is especially hard for her since the entire village of Highbury is buzzing with anticipation of meeting Miss Hawkins and since Mr. Elton is so well-liked by all.

e. Emma immediately feels that she will like him very much. She has been looking forward to meeting him for some time now.

f. Emma sees his plain satisfaction in seeing them together. A union between the two families (as Emma has already thought) would be a reasonable step. However, she is not by any means carried away by any fanciful notions of romance.

g. Frank has been acquainted with Miss Jane Fairfax.

h. Emma is now sure that Mr. Knightley was incorrect in his premature conclusions about Frank Churchill. She thinks that he is very sincere in everything he says and that he is not "acting a part" (p. 179).

i. Frank immediately fixes upon the idea of it being an excellent building for a ball. He doesn't mind the poor location of the place, nor its being considered somewhat of a lower class facility. Like his father, he is very enthusiastic, always light-hearted and very sociable.

j. Emma thinks he does not quite have as much pride in his social position as he should. In blurring the strong caste distinctions, he shows to Emma a certain "inelegance of mind" (p. 181), or so she feels.

k. Frank is certainly not complimentary, which stands out because of everyone's flattering style of speaking of everyone else. He seems rather quick to point out Jane's deficiencies as well as quick to agree with Emma when she does so.

l. Emma feels that Frank will marry for love and will look for a woman with excellent womanly attributes, with much less attention to things like money. Emma feels that this was the sole impetus behind Mr. Elton's engagement.

2.

b. Emma thinks it very rash and impetuous. He acted without giving thought to the feelings of his father and his wife. Traveling sixteen miles just for a haircut seems silly and immature. Mr. Knightley feels similarly, though more severely.

c. The Coles are quite wealthy, second in fortune only to the Woodhouses. However, they are rather nouveau riche, and their origins are much lower. Importantly, they are considered "only moderately genteel" (p. 188). Emma considers them much below herself and Mr. Knightley and the Westons.

d. Emma originally determines not to accept the inevitable invitation from the Coles, but when she does not even receive an invitation and when she hears that the Bateses, Harriet, and Frank shall attend, "those whose society was dearest to her" (p. 189), she becomes almost frustrated that she has not received an invitation. When the invitation does arrive (the lateness was due to the Coles awaiting the arrival of particular comforts for Mr. Woodhouse—his reputation for caution and complete serenity is well-known), Emma is quickly persuaded to accept. The Coles' thoughtfulness is used as an excuse for her change of mind.

e. The "less worthy" guests—Miss Bates, Jane Fairfax, and Harriet—are not invited to dinner, only to the party afterwards.

f. Jane and the Bateses have determined that the elegant piano is a surprise gift from Colonel Campbell.

g. Emma surmises Mr. Dixon (the new husband of Jane's good friend, formerly Miss Campbell) sent the piano. She suspects that he has fallen in love with Jane (which is why Jane has come to Highbury instead of vacationing with the Dixons in Ireland). Mr. Dixon has always been a huge supporter of Jane's musical endeavors, and, apparently, he once saved her from falling overboard at a water party—an easily romanticized moment, to be sure. Frank wholeheartedly agrees with all that Emma says.

h. Mrs. Weston, who heard from Miss Bates that Mr. Knightley volunteered his carriage to take them home that night, suggests a match between Jane Fairfax and Mr. Knightley. Mr. Knightley always spoke very highly of Jane as well.

Mrs. Weston even wonders if the piano is a gift from Mr. Knightley himself. Emma rebels against all such idea. She also notes that Mr. Knightley never does anything mysterious, such as give an anonymous gift (we have previously discussed his preference for straight-forwardness). Mr. Knightley confirms this by telling Emma of his disdain for the manner in which the gift was given.

i. Harriet worries endlessly over which cloths and ribbons to buy and whether to send her materials in two parcels or one and to send it to Mrs. Goddard's or Hartfield. Harriet very rarely can make up her mind about anything without the input of Emma and is very capricious. Her dependence on Emma is a major fault.

Miss Bates talks and talks and talks for a good part of the chapter. As Mr. Woodhouse has noted, she talks very fast and rarely can anyone else get in a word. She also has a rather annoying penchant for repeating verbatim the words and entire conversations of others. But, Miss Bates is well liked by everyone in Highbury on account of her sweet, self-effacing attitude.

3.

b. With Emma's theory about Jane and Mr. Dixon in mind, Frank baits her with pointed conversation about the gift and Colonel Campbell and "all that party" (p. 220)—i.e., Mr. Dixon.

c. Mr. Knightley is very direct, yet polite, with her. He makes his wishes clear.

d. Frank, like his father, loves a party and many guests and friends. With the help of Emma and the Westons, they come up with a list of people to invite to a ball to be held at Randalls. All the while, Mr. Woodhouse laments the inevitable sicknesses which would befall all of them were they to follow through on their plans for dancing. Randalls soon proves to be too small for such a party, and Frank again suggests the Crown Inn as the best place to have it.

e. Answer is up to you.

f. Mr. Knightley thinks it is foolishness. He has no desire to attend, although he will just to be polite.

Jane, on the other hand, is very open in expressing her pleasure at the idea. Because of his opposing something that she so eagerly anticipated, Emma is satisfied that Mr. Knightley has no romantic feelings for Jane.

g. His aunt, Mrs. Chuchill, becomes ill. She is known, however, to become ill at times convenient for herself.

h. Emma sees that Frank is strongly in love with her, and, although he wishes to tell her, he finds that she does not encourage such a confession.

4.

b. Emma realizes that, although she often thinks of Frank and wonders how he is doing, she is not unhappy without him. On the other hand, she is quite convinced that Frank is thoroughly in love with her. Because of the Mr. Elton situation, she is determined to be on her guard against any word or action on her part that might be misinterpreted by him.

c. She tells Harriet that her depressive state only serves to remind Emma of the painful mistake on her part that led to the whole mess. While she stresses this as a secondary reason for ending her mourning ("for her own sake" is the primary motive), Harriet is, of course, horrified that she is causing any small amount of anguish for her friend. Emma later reflects on the genuine love that her friend has for her and realizes how much she returns those feelings.

d. Harriet feels that her obsession with Mr. Elton will now subside, and she seems to be sincerely happy for both groom and bride (not that Harriet is ever anything but sincere).

e. Emma thinks that Mrs. Elton is too vain, that she means to show that she is better than the rest in little Highbury, and that her breeding left much to be desired. Emma dislikes her familiar way of referring to people (later she calls Mr. Knightley simply "Knightley," a slight to which Emma takes great offense).

f. Mrs. Elton compares Hartfield to Maple Grove, the residence of her wealthy brother-in-law and elder sister (Mr. Suckling and Selina).

She probably wants Emma to know that she is accustomed to at least the prosperity and affluence of Hartfield.
She recognizes that Emma is of the highest class in Highbury and wishes to impress her and make a good acquaintance with her.

g. Mrs. Elton tells Emma that she was surprised to find how ladylike Mrs. Weston was, considering that she used to be only a governess. Emma is almost too dismayed by the woman's impertinence to reply. Mrs. Elton and Emma shall not be friends.

h. Mr. And Mrs. Elton are more open in their dislike of Harriet than they are of Emma. Since Harriet is of much less consequence in Highbury, she is a safer target.

i. Mrs. Elton is impressed with Jane Fairfax, and she seems intent on becoming her benefactress.

Emma is surprised that Jane would come out of her near seclusion at the Bates' for such an odious woman as Mrs. Elton.

j. Mr. Knightley seriously assures Emma that he had never thought of Jane "in that way."

k. Mr. Knightley says that Jane is not as open as she used to be and that her reservedness is not appealing to him.

l. Mrs. Weston tells Emma that Mr. Knightley is so bent on not being in love with Jane that he may be surprised to learn that he actually is.

1. a. Read Chapters 34-36 of Jane Austen's *Emma.*

   b. Chapter 34
   Emma feels obliged to invite Harriet to the dinner of Hartfield in honor of the Eltons. What is Harriet's reply, and why does this please Emma?

   c. Why is Emma worried about the unexpected addition of Mr. John Knightley to the dinner party? How does the news affect Mr. Woodhouse?

   d. Why do you think Jane is near tears when Mr. John Knightley kindly tells her that in the near future she will probably be as successful as he is?

   e. What does Emma surmise from Jane's determined walk in the rain that morning?

   f. Chapter 35
   For what type of work is Jane looking? How does she feel about it?

   g. Who is Mr. John Knightley's opposite in this group?

   h. Chapter 36
   Mrs. Elton tells Mr. Weston of her "horror of upstarts" (p. 284). How is this somewhat ironic?

   i. About what does Mr. John Knightley softly reproach Emma?

2. a. Read Chapters 37-39.

   b. Chapter 37
   Now that Frank is only nine miles away from Highbury, what event can take place?

   c. Chapter 38
   Emma sees that Mr. Weston has confided in many different people regarding the ball, and she decides that, although she finds fault in Jane's reticence, she also finds fault in this other extreme. What happy medium does she look for in a man?

d. What does Frank think about Mrs. Elton?

e. What terrible slight does Mr. Elton give to Harriet? How does Mr. Knightley make up for it?

f. What does Mr. Knightley think of Mr. Elton's rudeness? What does he tell Emma about Harriet?

g. Chapter 39
How have many of Emma's concerns been favorably worked out?

h. What has happened to Harriet that could make her "faint away"?

i. After things have settled somewhat, what does Emma begin to consider?

3. a. Read Chapters 40-42.

b. Chapter 40
What is Harriet's confession?

c. Harriet has a new love interest now, although she freely admits that she would never even hope for him to return her affections. Who does Emma suspect the mystery man to be? How is Emma careful to guard herself against interfering this time, and what is the only advice she gives her?

d. Chapter 41
What has Mr. Knightley been thinking about Emma, Frank, and Jane?

e. Mr. Knightley is so convinced that there is some trickery about. If you believe Mr. Knightley, the following question is in regard to the supposed tricks and conundrums of Mr. Frank Churchill.

Can you figure out what is actually going on in the confusing sequence involving Frank, Mrs. Weston, Miss Bates and Mr. Perry's horse?

f. Why is Emma embarrassed to tell Mr. Knightley what was meant by "Dixon"?

g. Does Emma agree with Mr. Knightley's thoughts on Jane and Frank?

h. Chapter 42
Where do Mr. Weston and Mrs. Elton plan on going, and why can't they go? Where does the party go instead?

i. What does Mr. Knightley do when faced with the prospect of Mrs. Elton issuing all the invitations to his house and party?

j. What are some of Emma's musings as she peruses Donwell Abbey?

k. Who is Emma surprised to see taking a walk together?

l. What is Frank's disposition when he finally arrives at Donwell?

4. a. Read Chapters 43-45.

b. Chapter 43
How do Emma and Frank act towards each other at Box Hill?

c. How do Mr. and Mrs. Elton respond to Frank and Emma's liveliness?

d. Frank asks Emma to find him a wife, saying, among other things, that she must be lively and have hazel eyes. What does Emma think of his request?

e. How does Mr. Knightley rebuke Emma for her treatment of Miss Bates? How does class figure into his reprimand?

f. How do Emma and Mr. Knightley leave each other?

g. Chapter 44
What does Emma resolve to do after the fiasco at Box Hill?

h. Where is Jane going?

i. What does Miss Bates say about the party at Box Hill the day before?

j. When Miss Bates tells Emma about Frank being recalled to Richmond, Emma begins to compare the fortunes of Mrs. Churchill and Jane Fairfax. What are her thoughts?

k. Chapter 45
What does Mr. Knightley do when he learns from Mr. Woodhouse that Emma has just been to visit the Bateses?

l. What sad news comes from Richmond? How does Emma see this as positive news for Harriet?

m. While Harriet's future seemingly improves, whose future is growing increasingly bleak?

5. Write two to three paragraphs focusing on Mr. Knightley. Although Austen does not often employ symbolism in naming her characters, she probably does so here. In your writing, explain what you admire about Mr. Knightley. In what ways does he operate nearly beyond class rules? How does he show his resolve and strong moral character? Describe his manner of interacting with all sorts of different people.

1.

b. Harriet asks not to come. This pleases Emma for two reasons: first, she sees that Harriet is capable of declining a request from her friend, showing more strength of character; and second, this enables Emma to invite Jane Fairfax, whom Emma preferred to have in the present company.

c. Mr. John Knightley is not very fond of parties and a lot of company, and Emma is worried that he will not be in a very good mood.

   Mr. Woodhouse is simply distressed because eight guests for dinner is about as much as his poor nerves can handle, and nine would make it difficult for him. Fortunately, Mr. Weston has to bow out of the dinner due to unexpected business.

d. At present, Jane is not in a very high financial position. Perhaps she worries about her life and future much more than she lets on.

e. Emma believes that Jane must have been expecting a very important letter from a person very important to her to have taken the trouble to walk to the post office in the rain.

f. Jane is looking for employment as a governess.
   She likens it to the slave trade, saying that the suffering of those prospective governesses is similar to that of slaves being bought and sold. While Jane says that she will be satisfied with any gentleman's family, she appears despondent at her prospects, and Mrs. Elton tries to convince her that she is quite worthy for a high-class family.

g. Mr. Weston. Mr. John Knightley is amazed that Mr. Weston decided to spend his evening at the small party after spending the whole day in London.

h. Mrs. Elton professes her disdain for people who are nobody in themselves, but latch onto the prestige of a family that they have been married into. Mrs. Elton seems to act this way often, with her constant referrals to Maple Grove and Mr. Suckling.

i. Mr. John Knightley is about to leave his two oldest boys in Emma's care, and he mentions that she may not have enough time for them, with all the society she is enjoying. His brother concurs, but Emma denies it, saying that she is rarely away from Hartfield. While she and Mr. John Knightley have opposing ideas about how much society one should enjoy, Emma is probably more correct in her assessment of her activities.

2.

b. The ball at the Crown Inn can take place.

c. Emma believes that she would cherish a man who showed "general benevolence, but not general friendship" (p. 292).

d. Like Emma, Frank does not like Mrs. Elton at all. He is also quite offended by her familiarity with Jane (to her husband referring to her simply as "Jane").

e. After telling Mrs. Weston he would love to dance with her and she recommending Miss Smith instead, Mr. Elton abruptly changes his mind about dancing and declines the offer.

Mr. Knightley soon becomes Harriet's knight-in-shining-armor and asks her to dance, although, as you recall, he has told Emma that he is not fond of balls or dancing at all.

f. Mr. Knightley is very angry with Mr. Elton, as well as Mrs. Elton for their treatment of Harriet. But he also suspects that their contempt for Harriet stems from Emma's earlier designs on Mr. Elton. He kindly tells Emma that he was wrong about Harriet and that Mr. Elton would have been better off with Harriet than with his present wife.

g. Emma and Mr. Knightley are in agreement about Harriet and the Eltons, Frank is not so much in love with her as he once was, and Harriet has given up her infatuation with Mr. Elton.

h. While Harriet walks outside of Highbury, she spots a band of gypsies. One of the children begs for money, and when she gives the group a shilling, they ask for more and more. The very idea of gypsies is quite enough to frighten Harriet and their crowding around her completely terrifies her. Frank comes to her rescue and brings her safely to Hartfield. (It is doubtful that the gypsies would have harmed her; they were only begging for money.)

i. As she reasons to herself, "[the situation] could hardly fail of suggesting certain ideas to the coldest heart and steadiest brain" (p. 306).

3.

b. Harriet has kept a few worthless scraps of nostalgia from when she was in love with Mr. Elton. She decides to burn them, to symbolically end her affections for Mr. Elton.

c. Emma knows that Harriet is thinking of Frank Churchill, because who else has taken her instantly "from perfect misery to perfect happiness" (p. 313)?

Emma tells Harriet not to even tell her who the man is, so that she (Emma) cannot be responsible for any blunders this time. She only tells Harriet to watch this man to see if he shows any sign of returning her affection.

d. Mr. Knightley is sure that Frank is pursuing Emma, but he is not sure why. While everyone else believes that Frank is in love with Emma, Mr. Knightley suspects that he might be only using Emma to mask another affection, a fondness for Jane.

e. Answer on your own.

f. While Emma still believes her theory about Jane and Mr. Dixon, she is ashamed to have revealed such a sordid thought to anyone, and is certainly too ashamed to tell it to Mr. Knightley who would certainly give her a fervid reproof.

g. Not at all. Emma congratulates Mr. Knightley for trying to use his imagination, but she assures him that, as she is in confidence with Frank, he has no intentions for Jane.

h. They plan on going to Box Hill for a luncheon party, but a horse comes up lame, and the whole thing must be put off.

Mr. Knightley volunteers Donwell Abbey as a place for the forlorn partygoers, and his invitation is accepted.

i. In true Knightley fashion, he firmly and calmly stands his ground and does not allow himself to be ruled by Mrs. Elton.

j. She is proud to be associated with the Donwell family (through her sister's marriage). She is very fond of the building and the surrounding gardens and lands.

k. Emma is happy to see Mr. Knightley walking and talking with Harriet.

l. Frank is very much "out of humor." He says it is because of the heat, and Emma is thankful that she is not in love with a man so easily upset.

4.

b. Although Emma had earlier promised herself to not give Frank any romantic encouragement, it seems she intends to enjoy his compliments and gallantry towards her. For her part, she has no romantic intentions whatsoever, but those others in the party (the Eltons, Mr. Knightley, Miss Bates, Jane, Harriet, and Mr. Weston) could only interpret the conversing as flirtatious.

c. They both sneer at their jovial manner, and make it known that they consider both Frank and Emma (especially Emma) to be very immature and rude. Certainly, Frank and Emma have been overly talkative for the company, but Mrs. Elton takes too great offense at not being the center of attention—Mr. Elton simply follows his wife's lead. They both leave the party. Emma regrets the poor mix of company.

d. Emma immediately thinks of Harriet, who has neither hazel eyes nor is very lively.

e. Mr. Knightley tells Emma that his privilege of telling her when she is wrong is often a burden rather than a privilege. Nevertheless, he expresses his displeasure with her blatant insult of Miss Bates.
He allows that Miss Bates is often preposterously talkative and dull, and if she were

Emma's equal (like Mrs. Elton), the affront could more easily be overlooked and understood; however, she is very much below Emma in class—in fortune, family, and future. Furthermore, the insult was given in mixed company—family (Jane) as well as the impressionable (Harriet).

f. Emma was too embarrassed and upset at her own bad manners to concur with Mr. Knightley as he spoke to her, and then she is upset with herself for allowing the two of them to part without even acknowledging his advice and concern. Emma feels genuinely wretched for her behavior towards Miss Bates and, particularly, for Mr. Knightley thinking so poorly of her actions.

g. Emma resolves to immediately begin her penance by visiting Miss Bates the next morning and to visit more often and on more equal terms than she had been used to doing.

h. She is going to be the governess for a Mrs. Smallridge. The family lives near Maple Grove.

i. Miss Bates says that the others may have seemed not to have enjoyed it, but she enjoyed it and feels "extremely obliged to the kind friends who included me in it" (p. 350). She is truly an angelic woman in spirit and seems to be sincere in all of her compliments, whereas others' compliments are, at times, contrived.

j. Emma sees that, compared to Mrs. Churchill, Jane is of no importance at all in the world, and she feels both shame for her silly speculations about Jane and sorrow for Jane's unwanted destiny as a mere governess.

k. Emma is pleasantly surprised by a gesture of "more than common friendliness on his part" (p. 354). Mr. Knightley takes her hand and seems on the verge of kissing it before he lets it go. Emma is not quite sure why he would stop at the last second and even less sure why he had begun at all, but she took great pleasure in seeing him perform such a gentle act.

l. Mrs. Churchill died. Although she was no one's favorite, she is finally given credit for having been as ill as she said she was. Emma sees her passing as new freedom for Frank to pursue Harriet.

m. Jane Fairfax's future is growing bleak. Despite her great talents and good connections, she seems doomed to be a governess for the friends of Mrs. Elton. Besides this, she has recently become quite ill and is unable to take any visitors. Or as Emma suspects, she is only unable to see Emma.

1. a. Read Chapters 46-47 of Jane Austen's *Emma.*

   b. Chapter 46
   Why are Mr. and Mrs. Weston so worried for Emma regarding Frank's shocking engagement?

   c. When Emma has regained her composure, what are her thoughts about Frank's deceit?

   d. Why had the engagement been kept a secret?

   e. Chapter 47
   Why does Emma remember Mr. Knightley's words "you have been no friend to Harriet Smith" prophetically?

   f. Why has Jane been so distant and uninviting towards Emma?

   g. What was the principal misunderstanding between Harriet and Emma, regarding the gentleman to whom Harriet was attracted?

   h. After the Elton affair, Harriet learned to be somewhat more cautious in her attachments. What two instances give Harriet the confidence to continue her affection toward Mr. Knightley?

   i. What regrets does Emma have about Harriet?

2. a. Read Chapters 48-49.

   b. Chapter 48
   Until talking with Harriet, what has Emma been taking for granted about Mr. Knightley?

   c. What does Emma tell Harriet in her letter?

   d. In what ways has Jane Fairfax been unreasonable during the period of secrecy?

   e. How has Jane's chat with Mrs. Weston made Emma even more depressed?

f. Chapter 49
Notice how throughout this chapter, there is no romantic indulgence, no flowery, foppish speeches, no fainting or excessive sighing. Austen describes her characters' feelings objectively, yet with real feeling. She has no need for silly, romantic devices used in other poorer novels of her time because she shows human emotion and the human thought process so well. The reader completely understands Emma's heady rapture and Mr. Knightley's profound relief.

How does Mr. Knightley feel about Frank now that he is engaged? How does Emma, now over the shock of it all, feel about Frank's behavior towards her?

g. What does Mr. Knightley say about Frank after he hears Emma's understanding words about him?

h. What are Mr. Knightley's fears before he speaks with Emma? What are Emma's?

i. Why did Mr. Knightley go to London in the first place? What did he find there?

3. a. Read Chapters 50-51.

b. Chapter 50
What two dilemmas still face our heroine, despite the utter joy she is now experiencing?

c. In his letter to Mrs. Weston, what does Frank tell her was his reason for giving the impression of attachment to Emma? Why did he feel it was somewhat acceptable to do this?

d. Frank recalls his unpleasant behavior towards Emma at Donwell, and later, his supposed flirtatious behavior toward Emma at Box Hill. He tells Mrs. Weston of something Jane said to him that day. What did she say, and what was meant by it?

e. How does Frank feel about Mrs. Elton? Why?

f. How does he explain Jane preparing to leave for the Smallridge's if she was engaged to Frank?

g. Who is the true bestower of the piano?

h. Chapter 51
After reading Frank's letter to Mrs. Weston, why does Emma think a little better of him?

i. What is Mr. Knightley's solution to the problem of Mr. Woodhouse?

j. How, according to Emma, is Harriet to be hurt by Emma's marriage?

4. a. Read Chapters 52-53.

b. Chapter 52
Why is Mrs. Elton so agreeable during Emma's visit with Jane?

c. Why does Emma think that Mrs. Elton may have been a little resentful towards Jane for the secrecy (and possibly for necessarily declining the position at the Smallridge's)?

d. How has Jane changed now that an open engagement is permissible?

e. Chapter 53
What is the new addition at Randalls?

f. Why do you think Mr. John Knightley was not entirely surprised by the news of his brother's engagement?

g. How does poor Mr. Woodhouse make out when he is told of the engagement?

h. After some reflection, what does Mr. Weston think of the news?

5. a. Read Chapters 54-55.

b. Chapter 54
How has Harriet's problem been abruptly and happily solved?

c. At one time Harriet misinterpreted Mr. Knightley's friendliness towards her (walking together and dancing). What were the reasons behind his actions?

d. What does Emma think of Mr. Martin now?

e. Recall the conversation amongst Frank, Mrs. Weston, and Miss Bates in Chapter 41. Can you explain the mystery now?

f. Chapter 55
How did Harriet come to love Mr. Martin?

g. Who is Harriet's father? Why was her parentage hidden? And why is her parentage still a blemish, despite her father's gentlemanly attributes?

h. Why must Harriet and Emma's friendship slowly become a close acquaintance instead of a close friendship?

i. How do Jane and Harriet differ in class? What contributes to the difference?

1.

b. They (as well as most of Highbury probably) have thought Frank and Emma to be at least slightly in love. They were both dreadfully sure that Emma would be devastated.

c. Emma is very indignant for herself, Jane, and her friends, the Westons. Frank's behavior towards Emma was quite improper and could have given her great pain if she had returned his supposed affections. She also immediately thinks of Jane and the position she has been put in. Although she was certainly party to the deception, she nearly accepted a position as a governess, of which she was apparently quite loath to accept. And of course, the Westons would have every right to be offended at the deceit of their young man.

d. Until the death of Mrs. Churchill, the union could never have taken place. The domineering, prideful Mrs. Churchill would not have consented to Frank marrying a woman who she saw as beneath him.

e. Emma, believing Harriet to be in love with Frank, is so distraught over her friend being futilely in love once again. She sees now that her best course would have been to tell Harriet to completely forget about him, that she truly had no chance of his returning her affections.

f. As Emma now realizes, she must have seen Emma as a potential rival for the love of Frank.

g. Emma imagined Harriet spoke of Frank, because he saved her from the gypsies. The rescue that Harriet referred to, though, was Mr. Knightley's gallant deliverance of her at the ball.

h. There was the walk Harriet and Mr. Knightley took together during the strawberry party at Donwell. And also, before Mr. Knightley left for London, he stayed and talked with her for nearly half an hour.

i. Emma regrets that she ever interfered with Harriet's affections. She is sorry that she made her think more of herself than she ought. Emma is not wishing that she had never befriended Harriet, only that she had listened to Mr. Knightley's advice about her. She feels that she has made Harriet a little too vain, perhaps a little too presuming for her own good (or for Emma's own good).

2.

b. Emma had not realized how important it was for her to be placed above the rest of Highbury in his affections. But she now sees that she has been blind and that Mr. Knightley does not hold her so high above everyone else as she imagined. The reproof at Box Hill is proof enough of this.

c. Emma asks her not to come to Hartfield for a while so that they might both forget the conversation they had about Mr. Knightley. Emma needs some time away from Harriet.

d. Jane feels that she was unreasonable in her frustration with Frank. She saw him being happy and carefree, while she was struggling so much with the weight of their secret, and she was probably somewhat intolerant of his easy way of dealing with the pressure.

e. Emma feels badly for not having tried to be friendly toward Jane more often. Emma has not treated her fairly in the past, and she regrets it now. She begins to wonder how soon it will be until the Westons begin to make a family, drastically reducing her role in their lives, and she thinks of how Frank and Jane would soon move away to Enscombe, leaving her alone with her father. If Mr. Knightley were to leave them too, she would be completely wretched.

f. Mr. Knightley is very upset with Frank. As we know, he very much disdains any secrecy or trickery in a man, and he is doubly upset because of the (as he sees it) trap that Frank placed for Emma—drawing her into his affections only as a cover for his own devices.

Emma, however, now sees that Frank never intended her any emotional harm. He only wanted to appear gay and unattached to anyone. Emma realizes her good fortune in not being enticed, however unintentional it was.

g. Mr. Knightley immediately begins to acknowledge that he has, perhaps, been mistaken in his quick judgment of Frank's character.

h. Mr. Knightley fears that Emma is distraught over the engagement between Frank and Jane.

Emma is afraid that Mr. Knightley is going to tell her of his love for Harriet. Their fears are disproved. This is truly a delightful chapter!

i. Mr. Knightley went there to get away from Emma, to try to forget about her. Recall that his last meetings with her were not very favorable to him. He witnessed her vain, flirtatious behavior with Frank and also found it necessary to reproach her for her treatment of Miss Bates. He felt little chance of her ever returning his love.

At his brother's house, he saw the happiness of married life that he so desired. When he learned of the engagement though, he quickly returned to Highbury to see how Emma was taking the news. "He had found her agitated and low. Frank Churchill was a villain. He heard her declare that she had never loved him. Frank Churchill's character was not desperate. She was his own Emma, by hand and word, when they returned into the house; and if he could have thought of Frank Churchill then, he might have deemed him a very good sort of fellow" (p. 398).

3.

b. Emma's main concern is her father. She is certain that she can never leave him. She is not so sure what to do about Harriet though. She decides to have her invited to her sister's house in London, so that they can have some time apart until she can be sure of what to say to her.

c. Frank needed a façade to hide behind. He believed that this deception was permissible under the circumstances because, although everyone else suspected mutual attraction, he was assured that Emma had no feelings for him. He even believed that Emma had pretty much discovered his entire plan.

d. After Frank makes a trivial comment about the brief acquaintance between Mr. and Mrs. Elton before they were married, Jane replies, "Such things do occur, undoubtedly…I was only going to observe that though such unfortunate circumstances do sometimes occur both to men and women, I cannot imagine them to be very frequent. A hasty and imprudent attachment may arise—but there is generally time to recover from it afterwards. I would be understood to mean, that it can be only weak, irresolute characters (whose happiness must be always at the mercy of chance), who will suffer an unfortunate acquaintance to be an inconvenience, an oppression for ever" (p. 342). She is telling Frank, in no uncertain terms to him, that any possible relationship he may have with Emma is demeaning to his character but may also be repented of.

e. Frank dislikes Mrs. Elton very much, because of her extremely condescending attitude towards Jane. He is especially indignant of her continuous reference to her as simply "Jane." He tells Mrs. Weston to note that even he has not yet referred to his fiancée by her Christian name.

f. Here is Frank's greatest blunder of all, yet it was his only unintentional one. Jane wrote to him to rescind the engagement because of excessive distress (mainly on her part). Upon receipt of the letter, he immediately writes her back, assuring her that things would now begin to drastically improve with the death of his aunt. Assured himself of her knowledge of his mind and love for her, he is shocked when he receives all his letters to her, returned, as well as a letter from her telling him that she takes his silence as agreement in the annulment. He realizes that he had never sent the letter, and decides to throw off the charade and talk to his uncle about everything.

g. Mr. Frank Churchill, of course, is the true bestower of the piano.

h. Emma is in such a charitable mood herself, and she sees how sorry Frank is, how kind he is to Mrs. Weston, that she does not see any need to continue to be angry with him.

i. Instead of Emma and her father moving to Donwell, Mr. Knightley suggests that he (Mr. Knightley) move to Hartfield.

j. Firstly, Harriet is infatuated with Mr. Knightley. Secondly, she would be losing her dear friend to marriage. Also, she would not be as free to come to Hartfield whenever she liked. Emma knows that Harriet will find another love interest eventually, but even Harriet could not "be in love with more than three men in one year" (p. 414).

4.

b. Mrs. Elton believes herself to be in deep confidences with Jane regarding her soon-to-be-announced engagement. She is very foolish to believe that Emma would not know about it, since Emma is so intimate at Randalls.

c. Emma surmises this when Miss Bates comes in and greets Mrs. Elton so warmly. Miss Bates does not like to have a quarrel with anyone. Recall how gracious she was to Emma after Emma had been so rude to her the previous day.

d. Jane is more open with her words to Emma, more amiable, and happier. She is so desperate to apologize to Emma for any slight or meanness, so desiring to begin a real, warm friendship, and Emma is also eager to apologize for herself.

e. The Westons had a baby girl.

f. Mr. John Knightley surely saw a change in his brother when Mr. Knightley stayed with them. This would be one of the few instances where Mr. Knightley is not entirely in control of himself and aware of his emotions. He is so confused about what he should do about his love for Emma that he behaves somewhat outside of his controlled character.

I only point this out to show you how carefully and delicately Austen creates and molds her characters. They are anything but flat characters. They are not at all constrained by stiff personalities that allow them no room for irrational or uncommon behavior. They are very true to life.

Consider also Emma losing her temper with Miss Bates at Box Hill. Or think how Harriet's character slowly changed, almost imperceptibly, over time. When she tells Emma of her feelings for Mr. Knightley, she is not quite the flighty, excitable girl who was so infatuated with Mr. Elton (although Harriet is not so well rounded a character as Emma or Mr. Knightley).

g. Mr. Woodhouse tries to remind Emma of her former strict stance on marriage, and he shows her examples of women who have suffered under marriage—poor Isabella and poor Mrs. Weston.

h. Mr. Weston wonders that he never struck upon it himself..., which brings up an interesting point—did you ever consider the match throughout the novel? As with Mr. Weston, it seems a very logical match, but Austen's heroine is so busy with other couples and a brief romance herself, that it is not easy to predict the outcome of the novel.

5.

b. Harriet has accepted Mr. Robert Martin's second proposal. Unlike the match between Emma and Mr. Knightley, this match seemed destined from the beginning, and it was only a question of when it might occur.

c. Mr. Knightley simply wanted to get to know Harriet better, for both Emma's sake and for Mr. Martin's.

d. Emma does not look down upon him as she once did. In fact, she very much looks forward to meeting him and making his acquaintance. As she told Mr. Knightley, "at that time I was a fool" (p. 436). She is not so haughty and superficial as she once was.

e. Frank brings up the topic of Mr. Perry and the obtainment of a carriage to Mrs. Weston. The confusion begins when Mrs. Weston denies any knowledge of any carriages, and Miss Bates chimes in, saying that she was one of only a very select few who knew about the carriage at all. Frank had heard of Mr. Perry acquiring a carriage from Jane in a letter (Jane had heard it from Miss Bates). Frank brought up the subject, thinking that he had heard it from Mrs. Weston.

f. After Harriet left Highbury, she soon realized that her attraction for Mr. Knightley was once more only self-deceit and brazen presumptuousness. This is a very positive step for Harriet, to come to that decision entirely on her own. Very fortunately for her, she is no longer dependent on Emma. She soon returned her affections to Mr. Martin.

g. Her father is a well-off tradesman.

He has kept himself hidden, only providing money for her care and upbringing, because she is still an illegitimate daughter.

Because of this and since Harriet is neither wealthy nor of very high-class descent, a match with her for any of the gentlemen of the high class of Highbury would have been a disgrace.

h. Mr. Martin is an employee of Mr. Knightley, and so, the two couples are of completely different classes. They will still visit from time to time, but their friendship will necessarily be less than the friendship of Emma and Mrs. Weston. This is simply the way of the world in early nineteenth century England. Both sides understand how things must be, and both sides accept it willingly.

i. Although neither Harriet nor Jane comes from particularly high standing families (Harriet much more so), Jane's parents were of fair standing in the Highbury community, though not particularly high class. Most importantly, Jane is

**considered to be higher in class because of her education and complete upbringing. Her upbringing allowed her to be eligible for a respectable status in society; even as the governess of a high-class family, she would be more respectable than Harriet. Everything about Jane, from her musical ability to her soft air of gentility, shows her to be of a much higher class than sweet, harmless Harriet.**

This week, write a five hundred word essay (about two typewritten pages double-spaced) on one of the following topics:

a. nineteenth century England's social caste system
b. women's role in nineteenth century England
c. detailed character descriptions of major characters, replete with quotations from text

Use the following guidelines when writing your essay.

1) The essay should consist of an introductory paragraph, body paragraphs, and a concluding paragraph.
2) Introductory paragraph:
   state the purpose of your paper in a clear and concise manner
   include a thesis statement
3) Body paragraphs:
   include at least three body paragraphs
   each paragraph must contain a clear topic sentence
   every sentence must support the topic sentence
4) Concluding paragraph:
   summarize the ideas of the paper
   opinions are given, if applicable

# *Essay Assessment II*

To help you assess your student's essay, complete the following checklist.

The essay contains:

1) a thesis statement that clearly identifies the main idea ________

2) an introductory paragraph ________

3) body paragraphs that support the main idea ________

4) a concluding paragraph ________

5) a topic sentence for each paragraph ________

6) sentences within a paragraph that relate back to the topic sentence ________

7) transitional words to relate one sentence to the next ________

8) a reworded thesis statement in the concluding paragraph ________

9) cohesiveness and unity ________

10) correct grammar, punctuation, and spelling ________

If your student has missed any of the above points, encourage him to go back and improve his essay. Congratulate him for his effort and completion.

# The Victorian Poets

1. a.

The Victorian Period

During the reign of Queen Victoria (1837-1901), Western Europe experienced the need to change while simultaneously resisting change. England, in particular, was being transformed by the enormous success of her industries and the accompanying scientific and technological advances. As farms became larger and more efficient, the agrarian lifestyle became a fond memory. The prosperity of the factories created an enlarged group of powerful people who were not necessarily born to a royal family. Furthermore, a large middle class emerged, from which anyone might distinguish himself and rise to the top of the social order in a country that had been accustomed to class distinctions. Democratic reforms aided this process as the monarchy was replaced by Parliament, and thus, traditional ways of life, traditional values, and traditional institutions all came under the strain of social and economic change.

The early Victorian period seemed to be rather optimistic and forward looking. Most Englishmen felt that the world was a good place to live and was getting better. Of course, improvements were still necessary, but they could be made with social reforms or scientific advances. In the midst of all this was the Man of Letters. These poets, novelists, playwrights, etc., were expected to comment on society in their works and provide moral instruction for the improvement of the reader. Thus, the Man of Letters was a moral and spiritual mentor, a teacher whose purpose was to poke our consciences while simultaneously entertaining us. Thus, since the writer was expected to observe his society, his writings reflected his social environment.

Most of the literature of the early and middle Victorian period reflected an optimism that things could be improved. The writer addressed his readers with the expectation that they would listen to him, and so his attention was directed at society. However, a marked change in this attitude occurred in 1859 with the publication of Darwin's *Origin of Species*, followed by his *Descent of Man* in 1871. In many people's minds, Darwin provided scientific evidence that discredited the Bible and the teachings of the church. The impact was profound. Of all the institutions that seemed stable in the continual change of this period, it was the church. A person could go to church and reinforce his beliefs in traditional values and traditional ways of life. After Darwin, however, people began to lose faith, question their beliefs, even their belief in God. A few felt relieved from the restraints of the church and from traditional societal pressures. Most people, however, were profoundly disturbed, and the latter Victorian period shows a marked pessimism and despair creeping into Western civilization. English writers reacted by showing pessimism about whether things were getting better. Some writers questioned or disregarded traditional values, and often turned their attention away from the condition of others and toward their own circumstances and feelings.

The major poets of this period were Alfred, Lord Tennyson, Robert Browning, and Matthew Arnold. Both Tennyson and Arnold were shaken by the changes that occurred in the Victorian Era. Browning, on the other hand, confronted the changes with courage and faith. Tennyson's writings are regarded as a sort of barometer of the period. His earlier poems are optimistic, but his tone turned more and more doubtful as time went on.

In form and content, the Victorian poets continued to break new ground, but they seemed to have little influence in terms of changing the way poetry was viewed. Browning, for example, did a good deal of experimentation with verse forms, but his experiments were not much appreciated. Arnold had the potential to initiate change, but he quit writing poetry rather early in his career and never accumulated the following he might have had. All in all, the Victorian poets reflected the age they lived in, being changed by events and discoveries of the era, but resisting and resenting the need to change with the times.

b. Poet's Corner

**Alfred, Lord Tennyson** was born in Somersby Lincolnshire, on August 6, 1809. One of twelve children, he wrote several poems and plays by the time he was fifteen years old. Due to epilepsy (thought to be shameful in those days) and heavy drinking in his family, Tennyson spent his entire life with the fear of mental illness. He entered Trinity College where he met Arthur Hallam, with whom he developed a deep friendship. Although their friendship was short, the loss of Hallam from an illness left Tennyson in a deep state of spiritual depression. He devoted the next ten years of his life to reading and meditation, refusing to publish any of his works. At the end of this time, the publication of his 1842 two volume *Poems*, which included "Morte d'Arthur," "Locksley Hall," and "Ulysses," established Tennyson as the greatest poet of his day. *In Memoriam*, a tribute to Arthur Hallam, is probably considered one of the greatest works in British literature. Tennyson suffered from severe nearsightedness that caused him to work on much of his poetry in his head for sometimes years. Tennyson's poetry was admired by Prince Albert, thereby dedicating *Idylls of the King* to him. Later, Queen Victoria bequeathed Tennyson with his title. He died on October 6, 1892, at the age of 83.

c. Acquaint yourself with some of Tennyson's poetry. Try reading a poem aloud.

2. a. Read Tennyson's "St. Agnes' Eve," pp. 220-221.

   Note: According to an old legend, if a young girl performs certain rituals on the eve of St. Agnes' Day, she might be given a vision of her future husband.

   b. The speaker of this poem is not Tennyson. What place is the speaker referring to?

   c. What further clues to the speaker's identity are given in the last four lines of stanza two?

   d. Whom does the nun consider to be her future Bridegroom?

   e. In what ways would you consider this poem to have a positive outlook on life?

3. a. Tennyson's *In Memoriam* is a series of more than a hundred poems written over a period of seventeen years. The poems are dedicated to the memory of Arthur Hallam, a close friend

of Tennyson's who died suddenly at the age of 22. Hallam was engaged to marry Tennyson's sister, making the loss doubly painful. The impact of Hallam's death on Tennyson was great, shaking Tennyson's faith in God, the meaning of life, tradition, etc.

b. Read Tennyson's "Dark House, by Which Once More I Stand," page 232 and "I Envy Not In Any Moods," page 233.

c. In what form are these poems written?

d. Do you think an empty house is a good image to evoke the sense of losing a friend?

e. How does the time of day help to increase the emotional impact in "Dark House"?

f. Is "Dark House" uplifting or not? Does Tennyson deal with his loss in any positive way?

g. Is the message of "I Envy Not" positive or negative?

4. a. Read Tennyson's poem "O Yet We Trust that Somehow Good," page 235.

b. Compare "O Yet We Trust," page 235 with "I Envy Not," page 233. What is the difference between the two poems regarding Tennyson's outlook on life?

c. How does the image of the infant reinforce Tennyson's uncertainty?

d. Read Tennyson's "Ring Out, Wild Bells, to the Wild Sky," page 238.

e. In the poem "Ring Out," what do we infer about the condition of English society at the time this poem was written?

f. The last stanza of "Ring Out" shows a significant difference from "O Yet We Trust" regarding Tennyson's faith. What is it?

5. Find a quiet spot today and spend some time writing your own poetry.

2.

b. The speaker is referring to a convent.

c. The speaker is deeply religious. The speaker is female. Since she apparently lives in a convent, the speaker is a nun.

d. She considers Christ to be her future Bridegroom.

e. First of all, the natural setting of the poem is described in glowing terms. The nun is excited by the snow, the heavens bursting with stars, the ground shining, etc. More importantly, the poem is full of faith. There is no doubt here, that the nun, who is young, looks forward to her remaining life with faith and optimism.

3.

c. Quatrains, consisting of iambic tetrameter with a rhyme scheme of abba. This is a regular form that has only traditional aspects.

d. Our sense of place is one of our most powerful human needs and leaving that place evokes powerful emotions. Our living space tends to reflect our personalities and always represents us some way.

e. The darkness before dawn is said to be the darkest hour. Also, it is likely that Tennyson is the only person on the street at such an hour, increasing the sense of loneliness.

f. Yes and no. In the last stanza, we get the impression that he is resolved to go on with life, but he obviously feels rather gloomy about it.

g. The message is positive. Tennyson takes something tragic and turns it into something good. The poem was probably written with his sister in mind.

4.

b. "I Envy Not" is very certain about taking tragedy as a part of life (and seeing the good in it). "O Yet We Trust" shows a good deal of doubt about this.

c. The infant doesn't know if it will be heard or not. If heard, he still doesn't know when a response will come and can't communicate what he wants when a response does come. This poem is full of doubt. Tennyson seems to feel that God is far from him.

e. Since there are so many undesirable things to be rung out, we surmise that English society is far short of Tennyson's hopes for it.

f. "O Yet We Trust" shows Tennyson trying to obtain faith from within himself, but failing. "Ring Out" shows a bleak outlook on society, but faith for its improvement is in Christ.

1. a. Poet's Corner

   **Robert Browning** was born in London, England, on May 7, 1812. The story of his marriage to Elizabeth Barrett is probably as well-known as his poetry. She was a semi-invalid who was tightly kept by an overprotective father. Nevertheless, their relationship developed, and they finally eloped to Italy. Elizabeth regained her health, and they enjoyed a happy marriage until her death in 1861. Browning would live another 28 years, and he would continue writing with excellence despite his loss.

   Robert grew up in a family that instilled deep religious thinking and a love for literature, painting, and music. Perhaps this explains how he succeeded without any formal education after he was fourteen years old. Understandably, Browning's poetry before Elizabeth's death shows a good outlook on life. However, even after she was gone, his poetry did not diminish in its message of faith, courage, the belief in right vs. wrong, and the certainty that life's course was to be reconciled with God. Furthermore, Browning confronted Darwin rather than being confused by evolution. One might say that Browning reacted to the changes occurring in the Victorian era but was not much changed himself. Although his dramatic poem, "Paracelsus," in 1835 caused his literary peers to take notice, it was not until 1869, when he published *The Ring and the Book* that brought him widespread fame. Robert Browning is best known for his understanding of the human personality and his artistic ability to create dramatic monologue. He died on December 12, 1889, in Venice and was buried in Poet's Corner, Westminster Abbey.

   b. Acquaint yourself with some of Robert Browning's poetry. Try reading at least one poem aloud.

   c. Begin writing poetry today. Try different rhyme schemes. Remember to avoid clichés. You will have time the next couple of days to complete the poem.

2. a. Read Robert Browning's "Home–Thoughts From Abroad," page 257.

b. Do you see a regular form to this poem? Consider rhyme, meter, line length, number of lines, etc.

c. Is there anything unusual about the subject matter of this poem?

d. Read Browning's "My Last Duchess," pp. 266-267.

e. What is the form of the poem?

f. Count the lines in the poem and mark with a pencil, lines 13, 21, 24, 34, 43, 47, 53. What change do you see in the speaker's attitude beginning in line 13?

g. From lines 21-34, what are the prevailing attitudes of the speaker?

h. What happens between lines 34-47?

i. Lines 49-53 give clues as to the Duchess' demise. What are the clues?

j. Is there a moral lesson in this poem?

k. Continue working on your poem, if necessary.

3. a. Find Robert Browning's poem, "Rabbi Ben Ezra", pp. 275-279. Read the first stanza and the last eight stanzas.

b. This poem was written not long after the death of Elizabeth. How does Browning's reaction compare with Tennyson's reaction to the death of Arthur Hallam?

c. How does Browning apply the potter-clay metaphor to himself? List three things that stand out.

d. Is there evidence that Browning was a Christian in the sixth to last stanza (stanza 27)?

e. There are multiple meanings to the last line of the poem. Can you think of three meanings?

f. Continue working on your poem if necessary.

4. a. Poet's Corner

   **Matthew Arnold**, poet, historian, and critic was born in Laleham, Middlesex, in 1822. He attended a prominent school where his father was headmaster and later studied at the University of Oxford. As a professor, he also lectured in the United States. Arnold's poetry defines his philosophy in a plaintive, meditative tone. Matthew Arnold died in 1888.

   Some of his most famous works are "Empedocles on Etna" (1852), "Sohrab and Rustum" (1853), and "The Function of Criticism at the Present Time" (1865), a critical essay. His struggle with traditional religion is evidenced in the following lines from "Stanzas from the Grande Chartreuse" (1855):

   > Wandering between two worlds, one dead,
   > The other powerless to be born,
   > With nowhere yet to rest my head,
   > Like these, on earth I wait forlorn.

   b. Acquaint yourself with Matthew Arnold's poetry. Read some of his poetry; try reading one aloud.

5. a. Read Matthew Arnold's "Dover Beach," pp. 298-299. The poem is about one's loss of faith, presumably Arnold himself, perhaps after being convinced that Darwin's theory of evolution is true. Notice also that the speaker is addressing someone else in the poem—his love—mentioned in the last stanza.

   b. What mood is created in the first six lines?

   c. How does line 9 change the mood?

   d. In stanza two, "the turbid ebb and flow of human misery" suggests that mankind is awash in a sea of misery. How would you elaborate on the metaphor? What is it like for us to be in a sea of misery?

   e. In stanza three, *girdle* means encircle, and *shingles* are pebbles. What overall effect does loss of faith seem to have on the poet?

   f. In the last stanza, what does life hold for Arnold without his faith?

2.

b. Although there is a rhyme element, it is not in any regular pattern. The iambic meter is not much more evident than we find in normal language. Line length and stanza are both irregular. This form has both traditional and modern aspects to it.

c. Not really. This is what many people think a poem should be—inspirational and uplifting.

e. The poem contains heroic couplets.

f. He appears to be jealous of anyone else who could please his wife.

g. He is very critical, displeased, jealous, and proud.

h. The speaker tries to correct her, but she won't listen. He finally issues ultimatums, after which she dies, but we are not told how this happens.

i. The speaker's preoccupation with the dowry seems very important to him. The marriage appears to be a means of securing more possessions. Love is not mentioned; the girl is only his "object." Perhaps the last duchess was done away with so that her possessions could be retained and the next dowry obtained.

j. The poem was written with an actual person, the Duke of Ferrara, in mind. Browning is warning us that such evil is something we all need to occasionally be aware of in others, and perhaps to some extent in ourselves.

3.

b. Tennyson was badly shaken. He questioned his faith, the existence of God, the meaning of life, etc. Browning reconciles the tragedy with God's overall plan for his life and derives meaning from the experience by pressing into the Lord.

c.

1) Since God gives us each day of our lives, Browning resolves to make the best of each day without letting the past drag him down.
2) Although our circumstances change, God and our relationship with God do not change.
3) God uses our circumstances to help build and shape us.

d. "What entered into thee/That was, is, and shall be:" seems to be a reference to the salvation experience.

e.

1) We should live our lives as best we can right to the last.
2) As we look back on our lives, we should be able to say that we did the best we could under all circumstances.
3) As we grow older, we should show tolerance and patience with young people, since we have experienced much of what they go through.

5.

b. The mood is peaceful, quiet, and pleasant.

c. The exclamation point after

"Listen!" interrupts the mood. Furthermore, the sound of waves on the beach, which is generally considered relaxing, is a "grating roar" to the speaker. Notice that by the end of the stanza, the poem has gone from a pleasant mood to an "eternal note of sadness."

d. First, the poem suggests that misery, like the sea, is something that is always with us, permanent and part of life. Secondly, "turbid" gives an impression of buffeting, as if it is out of our control. Although misery can ebb for a season, "ebb and flow" suggests that reprieves from all misery are only temporary. Whew! At least we're not drowning in it, but Arnold depicts us with heads just above water.

e. He finds it depressing.

f. Answers may vary.

a. For your next writing assignment, you will write a 500-600 word essay (about two to three typewritten pages, double-spaced), giving your interpretation of Matthew Arnold's "Dover Beach" on page 298. You will have one week to complete the essay. "Dover Beach" is a good subject for an essay because it can be separated into three manageable paragraphs.

b. Let's return to stanza one of "Dover Beach" and examine it more closely. Consider the natural objects in Arnold's first eight lines. We have the sea, the moon, the cliffs of Dover, the bay, etc. All these things are permanent and unchanging. We are used to the expression about the inevitability of the sun rising. This is Arnold's variation of that saying. The sea, moon, and cliffs are going to be there every day without changing. It's something we can all count on. Lines 9-14 also show us something permanent and unchanging (according to Arnold)–"eternal sadness."

c. Stanzas two and three form a unit, in that they are both metaphors relating to the sea. We have found some points of comparison between misery and the sea, so look at stanza three. In my introductory remarks (Lesson 22, **5a**), I said that this poem might have been written with Darwin's theory of evolution in mind. Since the theory of evolution proposes an alternative to Biblical creation, perhaps the "sea" in this stanza refers to the waters of creation in Genesis 1-9. Our case for this can be strengthened by our interpretation of the words "round" and "girdle" to mean completely surround. We further must say that "earth's shore" is still under water, and has not yet been revealed. Therefore, Arnold's faith is like the waters of creation, shrinking and receding, leaving great holes—enormous gaps—where there was once an uninterrupted solidarity. The effects of this loss of faith are made clear in the rest of stanza four.

d. Now, let's try to organize some of this information. If we limit our introductory and concluding paragraphs to about 75-100 words, then we can make each body paragraph 125-150 words. For your first body paragraph, explain stanza one; for the second body paragraph, explain stanzas two and three; for the third body paragraph, explain stanza four. For your opening paragraph, introduce the poem and its writer, and expound on your interpretation of the main idea and mood of the poem. For your concluding paragraph, give your interpretation of the last two lines of the poem.

e. Let me help you with the first body paragraph. The central ideas of the first stanza are the peaceful setting, the images of permanence, and the transition from this to the disturbing eternal sadness. Your task is to introduce this with a good topic sentence, then choose perhaps two examples under each subtopic to illustrate your point. So, for images that suggest things that are permanent and unchanging, you might choose the moon and the cliffs and write a sentence or two explaining how each of these represents something that doesn't change. You will have to create something here. For example, you can emphasize how the moon assumes its place every night, just like the sun does every day. The cliffs, likewise, have been there before men ever came to England, and make us think of strength and endurance, like the expression "solid as a rock." A rough outline for this paragraph might look something like this:

I. Stanza one begins with peace and security, but changes to a disturbing note of sadness.
   A. Things representing that which is permanent and unchanging.
      1. the moon
      2. the cliffs
   B. Things showing peace and tranquillity.
      1. "tranquil bay"
      2. the sound of waves on the shore is relaxing
   C. The disturbing note of sadness.
      1. the exclamation point
      2. the "grating roar"
      3. the "eternal note of sadness"

f. Having sketched an outline for the first body paragraph, the same should be done for the other two body paragraphs. Keep in mind that only a couple of examples need to be used, even though there might be several more that could be chosen. We want to choose examples that make the point, and leave it at that. So, for paragraph two, you would choose the two metaphors involving the sea and try to explain these in just one paragraph. Your outline might look something like this:

II. Stanzas two and three revolve around metaphors comparing human misery and faith to the sea.
   A. Human misery is compared to the sea.
      1. The sea is always with us.
      2. "ebb and flow" suggests that relief is only temporary.
   B. Faith is compared to the waters of creation.
      1. "round" and "girdle" might be interpreted as completely surrounding.
      2. This makes sense because Darwin challenges creationism.
      3. Faith recedes just like waters of creation.

g. Well, enough of this. Take about five days to write a complete essay according to the directions we have been following. You are on your own for the third body paragraph and for interpreting the last two lines.

# *Essay Assessment III*

To help you assess your student's essay, complete the following checklist.

The essay contains:

1) a thesis statement that clearly identifies the main idea ________

2) an introductory paragraph ________

3) body paragraphs that support the main idea ________

4) a concluding paragraph ________

5) a topic sentence for each paragraph ________

6) sentences within a paragraph that relate back to the topic sentence ________

7) transitional words to relate one sentence to the next ________

8) a reworded thesis statement in the concluding paragraph ________

9) cohesiveness and unity ________

10) correct grammar, punctuation, and spelling ________

If your student has missed any of the above points, encourage him to go back and improve his essay. Congratulate him for his effort and completion.

# A Tale of Two Cities

Teacher's Note: The beginning of this lesson includes a summary of the novel. This is designed to help you discuss the novel with the student. Also, some students are better able to understand the novel if they read a summary; however, it should not replace reading the full novel. Please note that any surprise element or suspense is revealed in the summary. Use the summary to best meet your student's needs.

Lessons 24-29 Novel Unit - *A Tale of Two Cities* by Charles Dickens
Published by the Penguin Group ISBN 0-14-043054-7

Lesson 24

1. a. Link to the Author: Charles Dickens

Charles Dickens was born on February 7, 1812, in Portsmouth, England. His early years were full of happy times, but when his father was imprisoned for debt, Charles was sent to work. These were tremendously difficult years for young Charles, and it was from these experiences that he penned many of his novels. With the onset of the Industrial Revolution, Charles wrote about childhood poverty, the lower class, and social injustices.

Dickens is one of the most gifted writers of all time. Many of his novels have been made into movies, such as *Oliver Twist*, *Great Expectations*, and the perennial favorite, *A Christmas Carol*. Characters from his novels, such as Scrooge, Oliver Twist, and Madame Defarge, have become household names.

*A Tale of Two Cities* was written toward the end of Dickens' career, and it shows many of his great skills in storytelling. However, critics do not rate it among his masterpieces, perhaps because it is a little too brief to allow for Dickens' gifts for character and plot development. Nevertheless, *A Tale of Two Cities* is among the most popular novels ever and serves as a good introduction to Dickens, as well as a good representative work of the Victorian period.

When Dickens died in 1870, he had written fifteen novels and several short stories. His tombstone in Westminster Abbey reads, "He was a sympathizer to the poor, the suffering, and the oppressed; and by his death, one of England's greatest writers is lost to the world."

b. Summary of *A Tale of Two Cities*

"It was the best of times, it was the worst of times..."

With these famous words, Charles Dickens begins his tale of those who lived in the countries of England and France in the fall of 1775.

Jarvis Lorry, an agent for the Tellson's Bank in England, is sent on a secret mission to Paris. His purpose is to find Dr. Manette, a physician who has spent the last eighteen years of his life in the Bastille. Dr. Manette's daughter, Lucie, accompanies Mr. Lorry on the trip after she learns for the first time that her father is alive. In Paris, Mr. Lorry and Lucie go to a wine shop owned by Madame Defarge and her husband. They discover that the doctor is deranged from his long prison term. His memory is gone; he is withdrawn, and only able to cobble shoes. Seeing Lucie brings back a faint memory of his wife, and he turns to Lucie for comfort. Dr. Manette returns to London where Mr. Lorry and Lucie hope to nurse him back to good health.

Five years later, Lucie Manette, her father, and Mr. Lorry find themselves as witnesses in a treason trial. The defendant, Charles Darnay, is a Frenchman living in England and making a living by tutoring. His comings and goings from London to Paris have brought suspicion upon him. Lucie is reluctant to give any information that will harm Darnay, but must testify that she met him on a boat returning to England five years ago. Darnay's lawyer, Mr. Stryver, brings about his acquittal by pointing out that his assistant, Sydney Carton, bares a striking resemblance to Charles Darnay.

Although Sydney Carton engineered the defense for Darnay, Stryver took credit for it. That is the way of Carton's life and he drowns his sorrows in liquor. Sydney Carton is in love with Lucie but knows that the courtship is hopeless especially since one of his rivals for Lucie's affection is Charles Darnay. Nevertheless, Sydney professes his love to Lucie and tells her that he would sacrifice himself for her.

In France, the aristocracy has continued to use up the resources of the country, fueling the fires of revolution in the poor. One such aristocrat, the Marquis St. Evrémonde, rides furiously in his carriage through the impoverished district and accidentally kills a child. After a few more cruel encounters with the poor, he returns to his mansion to find that his nephew, Charles Darnay, has arrived. Darnay, the assumed name of his nephew, tells Evrémonde that the whole aristocracy is corrupt and that he will relinquish his inheritance when his uncle dies. That night, Evrémonde is killed by one of the Jacquerie, a secret society of revolutionaries who plan and precipitate the French Revolution.

One year later, Charles Darnay marries Lucie Manette. On the morning of their wedding, Darnay reveals his true identity to Dr. Manette. The doctor spends the next nine days cobbling shoes again, but returns to himself after that with no memory of the relapse.

In the years that follow, Sydney Carton remains a friend to the Darnay family. Lucie views him as a deep and unfortunate man who needs their consideration. In time, the Darnays have a daughter, also named Lucie. Meanwhile, the citizens of France arm themselves and, led by the Defarges, storm the Bastille, kill the government leaders, impaling their heads on spikes. When the Bastille is invaded, Defarge searches Dr. Manette's old cell for some private reasons.

In the Defarge's wine shop more plans are made to get even with the aristocrats and their kind. Madame Defarge is tireless, relentless, and ruthless in her revenge. The Evrèmonde estate is burned down and the steward of the estate is imprisoned. When Charles Darnay hears of these events, he decides to return to France, believing that he will be safe since he had relinquished his inheritance. He is imprisoned upon his arrival to Paris.

When Lucie learns of Charles' departure to Paris, she, her father, daughter, and nurse go to France. Mr. Lorry is now at the Paris office of the Tellson's Bank so he is able to help the family get settled. Dr. Manette has influence with the revolutionaries because of his imprisonment in the Bastille and is able to keep Charles safe in prison awaiting a trial. However, since the fervor of the revolution is new he cannot obtain Darnay's release for over a year. During this time,

Lucie and her family stay in Paris.

At the trial, Darnay defends himself strongly, but it is Dr. Manette's influence over the jury that obtains his acquittal. Amidst the celebration, Lucie is still concerned for her husband's safety. Shortly after they return to their home, four men come to arrest Charles Darnay again. By this time, Sydney Carton has arrived in Paris. When he learns of the recent events concerning the Darnays he makes secret arrangements with a spy. The next day, Carton goes to Darnay's trial. Not only are the Defarges cited as Darnay's accusers but Dr. Manette is as well. Defarge had retrieved some hidden papers from the doctor's old cell in the Bastille that were read at the trial. Through the reading of the papers all learn that it was the Evrémonde twins who had jailed the doctor. They had commanded him to attend to two of their dying victims. In the course of that event, the doctor learned that the aristocratic brothers had killed the whole family, except one little sister. When the Evrèmonde brothers intercepted a letter written by the doctor about the incident, they had him imprisoned. With Madame Defarge as the foremost accuser, and single survivor of the murdered family, the jury finds Darnay guilty and sentences him to death as being the last of the Evrèmondes. Lucie faints, and Sydney carries her from the courtroom.

Sydney Carton makes himself known to the Defarges by going to the wine shop where he learns that Madame Defarge is planning to have Lucie's daughter and father killed. Sydney gives Mr. Lorry his passport and makes all the arrangements for Lucie and her family to go back to England. Through a prior deal, he is smuggled into the prison. He forces Darnay to change clothes with him, write a dictated letter and then drugs Darnay until he is unconscious. When Mr. Lorry arrives with the carriage at the appointed place, he finds an unconscious Charles Darnay there instead of Sydney Carton.

As Sydney Carton is taken off to die in place of Charles Darnay, he imagines that his memory will live on in the Darnay family. He also imagines that they will name a son after him, and that the son would be the person that Sydney could never be in his own life. As he walks the steps to die,

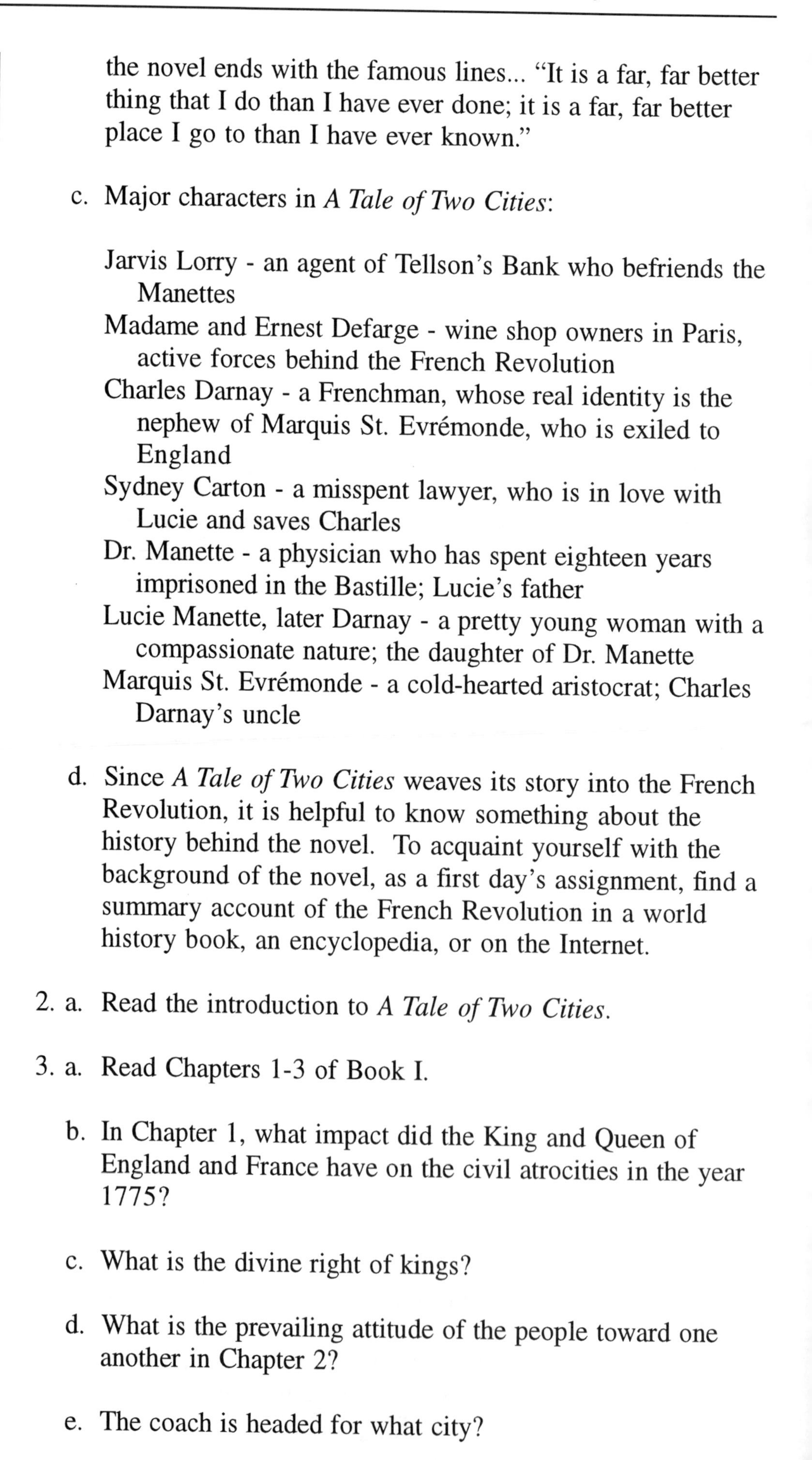

the novel ends with the famous lines... "It is a far, far better thing that I do than I have ever done; it is a far, far better place I go to than I have ever known."

c. Major characters in *A Tale of Two Cities*:

Jarvis Lorry - an agent of Tellson's Bank who befriends the Manettes
Madame and Ernest Defarge - wine shop owners in Paris, active forces behind the French Revolution
Charles Darnay - a Frenchman, whose real identity is the nephew of Marquis St. Evrémonde, who is exiled to England
Sydney Carton - a misspent lawyer, who is in love with Lucie and saves Charles
Dr. Manette - a physician who has spent eighteen years imprisoned in the Bastille; Lucie's father
Lucie Manette, later Darnay - a pretty young woman with a compassionate nature; the daughter of Dr. Manette
Marquis St. Evrémonde - a cold-hearted aristocrat; Charles Darnay's uncle

d. Since *A Tale of Two Cities* weaves its story into the French Revolution, it is helpful to know something about the history behind the novel. To acquaint yourself with the background of the novel, as a first day's assignment, find a summary account of the French Revolution in a world history book, an encyclopedia, or on the Internet.

2. a. Read the introduction to *A Tale of Two Cities*.

3. a. Read Chapters 1-3 of Book I.

b. In Chapter 1, what impact did the King and Queen of England and France have on the civil atrocities in the year 1775?

c. What is the divine right of kings?

d. What is the prevailing attitude of the people toward one another in Chapter 2?

e. The coach is headed for what city?

f. Where does Mr. Lorry work?

g. What conflict has been introduced, if any?

4. a. Read Chapter 4 of Book I.

   b. What is Jarvis Lorry's occupation?

   c. What is Lorry's connection with Paris?

   d. There are several things that connect Lorry with Lucie Manette. What are they?

   e. How does Lorry's dream in Chapter 3 foreshadow the news that Dr. Manette is alive?

   f. Notice Dickens' description of the setting. What is the dominant mood he sets?

5. a. Read Chapter 5 of Book I.

   b. Besides the foreshadowing of the blood bath to come, what does the people's response to the spilled wine show us?

   c. Mr. Defarge demonstrates some admirable traits, but what is his underlying response to Dr. Manette's long imprisonment and present condition?

   d. The implicit conflict in the story is alluded to on pp. 61 and 62, and represented by Dr. Manette's imprisonment. What is the conflict that will become evident in Book II?

   e. What could be the significance of Defarge's little league of Jacques?

3.
b. None. Neither did they seem to care much.

c. The divine right of kings is the belief that the king rules because he is born to it by God's will. As you might guess, this had a powerful effect on the king's opinion of himself.

d. The prevailing attitude is suspicion, guardedness, and other aspects of fear.

e. The coach is headed for Dover, England.

f. He works in Tellson's Bank, London.

g. We readers want to know the significance of "Recalled to Life," and Mr. Lorry's imagined unearthing of someone buried alive for 18 years. Otherwise, no conflict has been introduced yet.

4.
b. He works at Tellson's Bank, apparently managing a number of important accounts.

c. He services accounts in Tellson's branch banks in Paris.

d. Lucie Manette's father, Dr. Manette, was one of Lorry's accounts in Paris. Dr. Manette disappeared, presumed dead, and Mrs. Manette died not long after, leaving Lucie an orphan. Lorry took Lucie from Paris to London and placed her in a foster home. Dr. Manette has been found alive, so Lorry has been assigned to bring Lucie to him.

e. Dr. Manette has been missing for 18 years. It is as if he had been dead and were brought back to life.

f. The mood is gloomy. Everything is described in grim terms. Notice that Dickens likes to foreshadow coming events with descriptions of the setting, such as the buried reflection on the mahogany tables in Lucie's hotel room, and the headless cupids on the frame of the mirror (page 52).

5.
b. They are desperately deprived of life's necessities–food, clothing, etc.

c. He feels anger and deep resentment. We get the impression that this emotion could explode in retaliation.

d. The conflict is the miserable condition of the majority of French people, and the indifference of the French aristocracy. These are the conditions for a revolution.

e. It looks like some secretive group, like a terrorist group, or some other sort of revolutionary organization.

1. a. Read Chapters 1-2 of Book II of *A Tale of Two Cities*.

   Note: Be sure to read the footnotes, which are very helpful.

   b. How does Dickens compare Tellson's Bank to England?

   c. How does Jerry Cruncher's attitude toward his wife represent Tellson's Bank?

   d. How does the list of Tellson's condemned criminals reflect the condition of England?

   e. What evidence do we have from Chapter 2 that the charges against Darnay might be false?

   f. What is the general reaction of the people toward Darnay?

   g. Is there a conflict of any real substance yet?

2. a. Read Chapter 3 of Book II.

   b. Darnay's acquittal hinges on what important bit of evidence?

   c. How are Darnay and Carton unlike each other?

   d. What is the similarity between Darnay and Dr. Manette?

3. a. Read Chapters 4-5 of Book II.

   b. What is Carton's attitude toward Lucie?

   c. Does Carton like Darnay?

   d. Does Carton like himself? His life?

   e. We find that Stryver and Carton are old friends. Is their business relationship mutually beneficial?

   f. Why is Stryver called the lion and Carton called the jackal?

   g. Why does Carton insist that he doesn't think Lucie is much to look at?

4. a. Read Chapter 6 of Book II.

   b. What is the conflict between Carton and Darnay?

   c. What is the conflict between Darnay and Miss Pross?

   d. How do Mr. Lorry and Dr. Manette complement each other as a composite father for Lucie?

   e. What are the constant references to the multitude of footsteps bearing down on the apartments meant to suggest?

5. a. Read Chapters 7-8 of Book II.

   b. Why are the excesses of the Monseigneur and the Farmer-General so abominable at this time in France's history?

   c. Dickens goes to great length describing the attitudes of the people toward the Monseigneur. What does this show us about the Monseigneur?

   d. Defarge summarizes one of the points of Dickens' episode in which a child is killed. What is the point?

   e. What is another main point?

   f. Chapter 8 continues the displays of cruel indifference by the Marquis. Dickens foreshadows that this man will pay for his crimes. How does he show this?

1.

b. Both Tellson's and England resist changes in their laws and traditions, but both are badly in need of change.

c. Mrs. Cruncher's upright behavior convicts Jerry of his dishonorable conduct, but he reacts by trying to suppress the source of his conviction. He reinforced his posture by making an alliance with his son against Mrs. Cruncher.

d. None of the crimes were commensurate with the death penalty, but Tellson's obtained such convictions because the laws of England allowed it. In any case, the death penalty did not have to be given, but no mercy was shown.

e. Cruncher's reaction on page 90 is telling, since we expect a man of such low character to be indifferent. The narrator's own commentary on page 93 reinforces our suspicion.

f. They seem to be anticipating a guilty sentence and therefore a horrible execution that they apparently look forward to with pleasure.

g. The general conflict between oppressive ruling forces and their victims seems to be narrowing down to Darnay and his predicament. If Darnay's startled glance at Lucie Manette is due to a romantic link, then we are in for a real conflict.

2.

b. The fact that Darnay and Carton look so much alike forces the witness to admit he could very likely be wrong.

c. Except for their physical appearance, in every way, their characters are entirely different.

d. Both were imprisoned unfairly and then released. Cruncher understands that Dr. Manette has been recalled to life, continuing the resurrection theme.

3.

b. He is quite fond of her.

c. Apparently not; however, Carton helped to get him acquitted.

d. Carton does not like himself for what he has become (page 116). On page 114, he says "It (this world) has no good in it for me."

e. Yes. Stryver has no ability to organize, summarize, and prioritize the main points of his cases. Carton is good at this. Stryver is a go-getter who obtains the work, a skill Carton is unable to do.

f. Stryver is described over and over as shouldering his way to success. Stryver is well named because he strives to promote himself, and he is good at it. He is aggressive, like a lion. Carton, on the other hand, is weak in character and is a follower and a background figure. He thinks of himself as a rather low character, like a jackal, which feeds off the lion's scraps.

g. He is protecting his heart by trying to deny the truth.

4.

b. They are competing for Lucie's affection.

c. Miss Pross' "fits of the jerks" come on as a result of her fear of being displaced by Darnay.

d. Dr. Manette provides the loving father side, but is unable to be practical or protective, which is accomplished by Mr. Lorry.

e. Something horrible is going to happen, which will probably involve everyone in the apartment, since they all either heard footsteps or made remarks about them.

5.

b. In Western civilization, the two great sources of welfare for the poor are the church and the central government. Since a majority of French people were so in need of the basic provisions of life, the luxurious lifestyles of these people were particularly oppressive and abusive.

c. The Monseigneur has enormous influence and control; in short, he has great power.

d. The conditions for the peasants are so bad that it is better to die than to live.

e. Another main point is the complete indifference of the aristocracy to the peasantry's condition.

f. The Marquis is "steeped in crimson" (p. 144), as if covered in blood, in the glow of sunset. The crimson on his hands could mean his own blood and the blood of the peasants. "It will die out" has the same double meaning. Furthermore, the man on the road sees him dangling death-like from the carriage.

1. a. Read Chapter 9 of Book II of *A Tale of Two Cities*.

   b. We find that the nephew of the Marquis is Charles Darnay. What is the major difference of opinion between Darnay and his uncle?

   c. Who killed the Marquis?

   d. How does this chapter show us Dickens' opinion as to how the French Revolution came about?

2. a. Read Chapters 10-13 of Book II.

   b. Dr. Manette has a relapse of his prison mentality after Darnay asks for his daughter's hand. A clue to this is given on page 156 when the Marquis asks about a doctor and his daughter. What could the connection be?

   c. What is Stryver's motivation for being married?

   d. Does Carton have anything to offer Lucie that would be desirable in a marriage?

   e. Besides saying that he would give his life for her—a statement we really don't believe at this point—Carton displays a noble self-sacrifice in his dialogue with Lucie. What is it?

   f. Do the chapters involving Lucie's suitors heighten or decrease the conflicts involving the people who love her?

3. a. Read Chapter 14 of Book II.

   b. Based on this chapter and previous chapters, what is Dickens' representation of mob behavior?

   c. Where does Jerry Cruncher fit in with the mob in Chapter 14?

   d. How is the resurrection theme treated in this chapter?

4. a. Read Chapters 15-16 of Book II.

b. What is Defarge's main purpose for questioning the road mender with the three Jacques present?

c. Who keeps the list of people to be executed?

d. Who is added to the list after the road mender is questioned?

e. Why does Barsad reveal Charles Darnay's identity?

f. What is Madame Defarge's reaction regarding the information about Darnay?

5. a. Read Chapters 17-19 of Book II.

b. Lucie, Miss Pross, and Mr. Lorry all demonstrate a major theme in our story. What common characteristic do they show in these chapters?

c. Does Darnay's marriage to Lucie create any new conflicts?

d. Why does Dickens refer to the burning shoemaker's bench as the "burning of the body," and why are the tools, etc., buried as if "in a horrible crime" (p. 235)?

1.

b. Darnay knows that his uncle maintains the estate through oppression and cruelty. The Marquis feels this is practical and appropriate, whereas feels this is wrong and disgraces the family name.

c. Gaspard killed the Marquis. Remember, Gaspard is the man whose child was run over by the Marquis. Gaspard has joined the Jacques, the revolutionary force.

d. Dickens felt that the aristocracy kept its position by oppression, and it was indifferent to the people. The peasantry reached a breaking point, represented by Gaspard's taking revenge on the Marquis. In short, Dickens felt that the Marquis and the aristocracy brought the revolution on themselves. They got what they deserved.

2.

b. The Marquis had something to do with Dr. Manette's imprisonment.

c. Stryver's motivation is completely self-serving. Lucie is just a possession to be obtained for his pleasure.

d. Yes. He loves her.

e. Carton came short of asking her to marry him, which he would dearly like. He gave up the idea of marriage and was satisfied to just let her know that he loves her.

f. Both. Dr. Manette is very distressed after Darnay's proposal. Mr. Lorry and Miss Pross are also likely to feel a sense of displacement. On the other hand, the conflict regarding the suitors is settled, with Darnay receiving the blessing and Stryver and Carton stepping aside.

3.

b. The mob scenes take on a progressively lawless and violent nature. Dickens seems to show that mobs are dangerous and capable of almost any atrocity. In each case, the riots stem from deeply felt frustrations and are explosively released.

c. Although he joins the mob, he remains on the periphery, never really abandoning himself to the riot. Cruncher's association with Tellson's places him somewhere in between the middle class and the lowest class. His disgusting behavior, however, keeps him leaning toward the low class.

d. Cruncher and his son make a mockery of this theme, typical of their low character.

4.

b. He wants to determine the people who should be executed for having Gaspard publicly hanged.

c. Madame Defarge keeps the list.

d. The Marquis (St. Evrèmonde) and anyone related to him are added to the list.

e. He wants to see Defarge's reaction. Defarge's reaction to the news reveals his emotional conflict and shows Barsad that Defarge might well be linked to the Jacques who murdered the Marquis.

f. She is pleased to add him to her list. Madame Defarge is absolutely ruthless and is much more determined to get revenge than her husband.

5.

b. They show self-sacrifice. Each of them is willing to set aside personal well-being in order to assure Dr. Manette's well-being. Furthermore, Miss Pross and Mr. Lorry cooperate to protect Lucie.

c. Yes. Remember, Darnay is on Defarge's hit list. Defarge and his men will probably go after him, which will endanger Lucie's happiness, if not her life.

d. The shoemaker's equipment represents a personality that is assumed by Dr. Manette which is so strong that it is like another person–one that Manette knows of but cannot control. The burning and the burial are a symbolic destruction of this undesirable personality.

1. a. Read Chapters 20-21 of Book II of *A Tale of Two Cities*.

   b. Do we believe that Carton is serious about wanting to be friends with Darnay? Why or why not?

   c. In addition to the sense of triumph for the oppressed as they storm the Bastille, how does Dickens regard this event?

   d. How does the overwhelming of the Bastille increase the threat to Darnay?

2. a. Read Chapters 22-24 of Book II.

   b. What do you think the revolutionaries should have done differently to the Marquis' chateau?

   c. Among Darnay's reasons for going to Paris is his belief that he can help soften the fury of the revolution. Why do we know for certain this can't possibly happen?

   d. Would Gabelle have been pardoned if Darnay had stayed in France to manage the estate?

   e. The theme of death and resurrection now involves some members of the aristocracy escaping from death rather than the reverse. What other theme has taken a similar reversal?

3. a. Read Chapters 1-2 of Book III.

   b. In reference to Darnay's question about the decree, the postmaster replies, "There may be, or there will be. It is all the same" (p. 278). What does he mean by this?

   c. In the second paragraph on page 285, Dickens describes the prisoners as ghosts of elegance, wit, etc. What does this signify?

   d. Dr. Manette had some influence on the revolutionaries. Does he have enough influence to save his son-in-law?

   e. Are Lucie and her daughter in any danger?

4. a. Read Chapters 3-6 of Book III.

   b. Dr. Manette has become a folk hero, promoted to prison doctor. The circumstances have made him more active than ever. What ironies are apparent here?

   c. What impressions do the wood-sawyer, the Carmagnole, and Madame Defarge make on our opinion of Lucie and her daughter's well-being?

5. a. Read Chapters 7-8 of Book III.

   b. Are Dr. Manette's efforts to save Charles in vain?

   c. Why are Darnay's circumstances more hopeless than during his first imprisonment?

   d. Sydney Carton is capable of stepping out of his lowly character to show very high character traits. How do we know this?

   e. Do you find yourself growing in your affection for Sydney and wishing the best for him?

1.
b. You may answer this one for yourself. We have Carton's confession of love to Lucie. Now he wants to be friends with Darnay. Given his character, we have good reason to be suspicious. However, Lucie seems to see something genuine in him. I don't know what Carton is up to, if anything, but there is evidence on either side regarding his sincerity.

c. Dickens seems to say that there is no justice in mob rule. He represents the mob as murderous and bloodthirsty, bent on revenge, not justice. The mob is just as bad as the aristocracy.

d. The revolutionaries are armed and free to pursue him. The hanging of Gaspard is still fairly fresh in their minds.

2.
b. Completely destroying it was a senseless act of revenge. They could have plundered the chateau and taken what was useful to them, especially if there were provisions of food and money.

c. Darnay's name is on Defarge's list of people to be executed. His identity as the Marquis de Evrèmonde ensures his death no matter what he has done with the estate.

d. Not likely because Gabelle worked for the aristocracy and probably would have been imprisoned anyway.

e. The formerly oppressed peasantry have now become the oppressors.

3.
b. Darnay will be charged with something punishable by death. If there are no existing laws, something will be made up to convict him. It doesn't matter that Darnay helped the peasants rather than oppressed them.

c. He means that as the aristocracy are driven away, imprisoned, executed, etc., a way of life is also passing away. It is the end of an era.

d. Darnay is in Defarge's hands. Defarge knows that he is Manette's son-in-law, but Defarge has said that Darnay must die, regardless.

e. Defarge and the Jacques agreed that the entire Evrèmonde family must be exterminated.

4.
b. First, the imprisoned doctor has become doctor for the prisoners. Furthermore, he was useless as a prisoner, but now he is being used beyond all normal expectations for a doctor. Also, he is a life force in a death camp; his imprisonment, which was regarded as a death sentence, is the vehicle by which he is now able to save lives.

c. We are reminded how close she and her daughter are to being drawn into the revolutionary frenzy and put to death.

5.

b. No. Dr. Manette has prolonged Darnay's life for over a year. This is enough time for many things to happen which can still help Darnay. Without Dr. Manette's influence, Darney would have been lost long ago.

c. Having been rearrested means that Dr. Manette's influence was not strong enough to keep him free; neither were Darnay's own acts of goodwill. Furthermore, no one seems to escape the Defarges once they have made accusations against someone.

d. The best example is his confession of love for Lucie. He expects nothing in return except for an occasional visit. He blesses her marriage and even offers his help if she needs it. Not many people would do the same under the circumstances.

e. I think Dickens is hoping you will feel that way.

1. a. Read Chapter 9 of Book III of *A Tale of Two Cities.*

   b. Mr. Carton's conversation with Mr. Lorry, his observations while walking, and his repetition of John 11:25 show him in what process?

2. a. Read Chapters 10-11 of Book III.

   b. Dr. Manette's letter recalls the reason for his imprisonment, stating Charles' age to be only two or three at the time, making him completely innocent. Why is he still being executed?

   c. Do you think, as Charles' mother said, that Charles must make atonement for the families' sins?

3. a. Read Chapters 12-13 of Book III.

   b. At what point does Sydney Carton recognize that all hope for any alternative to his own plan is lost?

   c. How is Carton able to manipulate Lucie into leaving without seeing her husband to the last?

   d. Besides Barsad's help, how does Carton manage to switch places with Darnay?

   e. Is Carton a Christ figure?

4. a. Read Chapters 14-15 of Book III.

   b. The theme of death and resurrection asserts itself in several ways in the last two chapters. Can you identify the ones who are resurrected?

   c. What theme reappears when Madame Defarge dies?

   d. Do we see this theme return in Carton's vision at the last?

   e. Of all the characters in the book, who is the character that most illustrates a round character?

5. Today, you will begin a book review on *A Tale of Two Cities*. You will have all of next week to complete the assignment. (See Lesson 23.)

1.
b. He is examining his life before the end. He is preparing to die.

2.
b. Dr. Manette denounced the whole family, which reverses his previous testimony. Furthermore, the abuses of the Evrèmonde brothers were so horrible, that the people changed their minds, seeking to take revenge on any Evrèmonde who remained.

c. I think he has already made atonement by his benevolent actions. Atonement by taking his life is meaningless, except to have the satisfaction of revenge.

3.
b. When Dr. Manette lapses into his old prlson behavior, Sydney must proceed with his plan.

c. He convinces Lorry to take them away because their lives have been threatened by Madame Defarge. The only charge she needs is to condemn her for sympathizing with a victim of the guillotine (page 374). Therefore, Lucie can't show herself at the execution, and might as well leave as soon as possible.

d. He drugs Darnay. Remember his purchases at the chemist's shop (page 342).

e. No. He merely performs a Christ-like act.

4.
b. Perhaps all of them would have died if they had stayed. However, the people saved who had a death sentence on them were Charles, Lucie, and little Lucie. Also, although we might not be convinced that Carton was a Christian, Dickens wants us to believe that he dies and goes to heaven.

c. She gets what she deserves.

d. Yes. He sees Barsad, the Vengeance, etc., die by the guillotine.

e. Just about all the characters act along certain lines from beginning to end, except Sydney Carton. Carton shows a complex character that changes at the end of the story, making him the best example.

1-5.

a. This week, you will write a book review on Dickens' *A Tale of Two Cities.* Make your review about 700-1000 words long. Some of you will have trouble making your review this long. Most of you, however, will have trouble summarizing the story in a short enough length to allow space for the rest of the assignment.

Book reviews are required at just about every level of school, beginning about the fourth grade. Many teachers do not specify what they want from a book review, so our tendency is to summarize the content. However, this is only part of the task of reviewing a book. Requirements might vary, but most teachers like to see the following items appear in a book review.

b. First, identify the book by more than the title and author. Include information you would find in a bibliography. That is, include title, author, publisher, editor (if there is one), place of publication, and date of publication. Then, explain in general the overall content of the book in the opening paragraph. For example, in *A Tale of Two Cities*, you might explain Darnay's origins and his distaste for his family, causing him to leave for England.

You might say something about his life in England, his return to France, and certainly his predicament as a result of the French Revolution. You must not go into detail, but stay in the most general terms.

c. After your introduction, summarize the story. Identify main characters and what they do as you summarize. For books the length of *A Tale of Two Cities*, you should complete your summary in about five hundred words.

d. Once you have summarized the story, you should say something about major themes and what meaning the story might have. You don't need more than a paragraph or two for this. Be sure your examples are clear in this section.

e. Finally, write a paragraph or two about your opinion of the book. For example, if you liked or disliked the book, explain why. Perhaps the book was too difficult or easy, too academic, disorganized, anti-Christian, etc. Sometimes it is good to include whether or not you would recommend the book for further study or for others to read. Be careful not to offend your teachers with your opinions, if you can help it.

f. Once you have a rough draft, have your teacher read it. It doesn't matter if she has read the book or not. In fact, it is better that she hasn't read it. After she reads your review, ask her to tell you what the book is about in her own words, based on your review. If she doesn't do a good job telling you about the book, then you need to go back and revise.

# *Book Review Assessment I*

To help you assess your student's book review, complete the following checklist.

The book review contains:

1) title, author, publisher, place and date of publication ______

2) brief overview of the book in the opening paragraph ______

3) a summary of the story, including information identifying the characters ______

4) an explanation of the major themes, complete with examples or quotations ______

5) the student's opinion of the book, including his reasons ______

6) correct grammar, punctuation, and spelling ______

If your student has missed any of the above points, encourage him to go back and improve his book review. Congratulate him for his effort and completion.

# More Victorian Poets

1. a. Poet's Corner

   **Gerard Manley Hopkins** was born on July 28, 1844, in Essex, England. When he was studying at the University of Oxford, he converted to Roman Catholicism. He became a Jesuit novitiate at twenty-two and was ordained into the priesthood about ten years later. He studied theology in Wales, and there, by his superiors, he was encouraged to write poetry again. He held a professorship in Ireland and taught Greek literature. His artistic ability was evidenced also in music composition and drawing. While in Ireland, Hopkins encountered an extremely difficult time both physically and spiritually. He was overworked and became ill. Most of his work was not published until after his death. This accounts for his great influence on twentieth century poets such as T.S. Eliot, W.H. Auden, and Dylan Thomas. He died on June 8, 1889, from typhoid fever.

   b. The poetry of the late 1800's and early 1900's was expanding in form and content just like the novel. Moreover, as in the case of the novel, the changes were slight ones, because tradition still resisted anything too radical. The world was not quite ready for free verse, so poets tended to stretch existing forms, word choices, and subject matters. One of the more innovative was Gerard Manley Hopkins. Most of Hopkins' best poems remained within the accepted boundaries for subject matter. However, Hopkins wrestled with his faith, and wrote a number of poems that have come to be called the "terrible sonnets," in which his doubts are tormenting him. We have read poems by Tennyson and Arnold which tell of the pain of shaken faith, but for a priest to express such feelings was rather unheard of as a subject for a poem.

   Hopkins also experimented with word usage (diction). He sometimes invented new words or rearranged syntax to create innovative ways of saying a great deal in a few words.

   Although Hopkins experimented with forms, his most innovative invention was within the line. He used a method he called sprung rhythm. **Sprung rhythm** fixes the number of accented syllables per line, but does not count the number of unaccented syllables. Therefore, we might see in his sonnets a fixed number of five accented syllables. Although two lines might rhyme, one line might have nine syllables and its rhyming partner, thirteen. In this way, Hopkins varied the pattern within a line but kept the overall form. This reflected late Victorian society, showing a break from tradition while simultaneously wanting to maintain the old ways.

c. Read "God's Grandeur," by Gerard Manley Hopkins on page 349.

Note: *Foil* in line 2 refers to something like tinsel, which reflects light in all directions. *Reck* in line 4 is to perceive, and *rod* is God's discipline, or perhaps wrath.

d. Reread the first four lines. What is Hopkins saying in these lines?

e. What is the general message of lines 5-8?

f. Consider the two main points. First, Hopkins shows us that our magnificent natural surroundings point us to our Creator. Secondly, he shows that men fail to see this, and actually destroy the evidence that God has created. What else did God give us as evidence of Himself that we also destroyed, and continue to destroy or ignore even to this day?

g. How do lines 9-12 represent Christ's resurrection?

h. Begin writing poetry today and work on it throughout the week.

2. a. Read Gerard Manley Hopkins' "Spring and Fall," page 355.

b. Reread lines 1-4. What time of year is it?

c. What does Hopkins mean by "Leaves, like the things of man"?

d. What do lines 5-9 add to the poem?

Note: According to footnotes in the *Norton Anthology of Modern Poetry*, *wanwood* and *leafmeal* are invented words. *Wanwood* could mean that the trees (wood) are growing pale as their leaves drop. *Leafmeal*, which might be derived from leaf and piecemeal, suggests the dead leaves are scattered about.

e. Read lines 10-13. What is meant by "sorrow's springs"?

Note: *Ghost* in line 13 refers to Margaret's spirit.

f. What is meant by line 13?

g. Before we examine the last two lines, let's summarize the main points. Margaret is sad to see the leaves fall. She might not understand now, but she will someday, that death and dying are inevitable for her. The origins of sorrow are the same for everyone, and Margaret's spirit knows why, even though she doesn't.

Biblically, what is the origin of sorrow for the human race?

h. Read Gerard Manley Hopkins' "Pied Beauty" on page 351.

i. This poem is not difficult to understand, but you will enrich your appreciation for it if you look up any words you don't know. Furthermore, make a good effort to derive meaning from the unusual constructions, such as "couple-colour," and "Fresh firecoal." Note that "stripple" in line 3 is a misprint, and should read *stipple.*

3. a. Poet's Corner

**Thomas Hardy** was born in Dorsetshire, England, on June 2, 1840. The eldest of four children, Hardy was educated as an architect, probably due to his father's (a stonemason) urgings. He wrote poetry and later turned to novel writing. By the time he was about thirty-four, he was able to leave his profession and support himself financially through his writing. Although against his parents' wishes, he married Emma Gifford. After her death, he was inspired to write, *Veteris Vestigiae Flammae (Vestiges of an Old Flame)*, a collection of some of his best poems. He died on January 11, 1928.

b. Thomas Hardy is better known for his novels than for his poetry, although his poems are innovative and much anthologized. Hardy's poems tend to maintain traditional

[14] colloquialism: an expression acceptable in conversation and informal writing

form. Like Hopkins, however, he often distorted syntax and also created new words. Additionally, Hardy deliberately tried to make his diction more conversational than was conventional at the time, sometimes using colloquialisms[14] and deliberately avoiding words with flair.

Most unconventional was his subject matter. Hardy was pessimistic and skeptical, which gives many of his poems a grim, bleak tone. Although Hardy wanted to believe in God, he was never born again. Consequently, he developed his own world view.

Hardy felt that forces, which are outside our control, such as nature and natural law, are indifferent to us, unmindful of our human predicaments. He felt that a person could rise above his circumstances by acts of the will, but he also felt that fate could be unpredictable, cruel, and overwhelming. To reconcile these things, and to account for the spiritual forces that he sensed, Hardy proposed that there was an unconscious will or mind operating in the universe. This will, being indifferent to us, accounted for the conflicts we continually have with our natural surroundings. Thus, Hardy also reflects the late Victorian tension, in which the desire for tradition is strong, but the changing times cannot be held back.

c. Read "The Darkling Thrush" by Thomas Hardy on page 327.

d. This poem was written on the last day of the nineteenth century. At the end of the hundred year cycle, it was probably hoped that some spiritual event might take place.

   Note: In stanza one, a "coppice gate" is a gate that leads to a thicket. "Bine-stems" are the shrubs' intertwining stems.

e. What image is presented in stanza one?

f. What is the "Century's corpse" in stanza two, and what is it compared to?

g. What does the thrush represent to the narrator?

h. Consider that the thrush is a "Darkling Thrush." What are the spiritual overtones? If this poem were written by Shelley, what would you think?

4. a. Read Thomas Hardy's "The Oxen" on page 346. Note: The word "heartside" in line 4 is a misprint, and should read *hearthside*.

   b. This poem is about an old legend that tells of animals kneeling at the time Christ was born, just as they did at the manger.

   c. Why would the narrator say "So fair a fancy few would weave in these years!"

   d. Based on this poem and "The Darkling Thrush," would you say Hardy was hostile toward Christianity?

   e. What would you say to Hardy if you had the chance? He probably has heard all the intellectual apologetics and arguments regarding the reality of Christ.

   Note: Perhaps this would be a good time for you to write down your testimony and share it with someone else.

5. a. Read Thomas Hardy's "The Convergence of the Twain" on page 342.

   Note: *Thrid* in line 6, means *thread.* If you don't know the story of the *Titanic*, any history book or encyclopedia will have more than enough explanation for you. Be sure you have this information before you read the poem.

   b. Why is the sea-worm in line 9, "dumb, indifferent"?

   c. What is the "Immanent Will," line 18?

   d. In this poem, is the Immanent Will completely indifferent to human development?

   e. Let's say Hardy is consistent, and the Immanent Will is indifferent. What, then, would be his attitude toward the *Titanic* and what it represents of human nature?

1.
d. God is evident in nature (Romans 1). Hopkins asks, "Why don't people see this?"

e. People are destructive to their natural surroundings. Line 8 suggests that people have no regard for nature and just walk all over it without noticing.

f. God gave us Christ.

g. Spring is an old symbol for the renewal of life after death of winter. Notice that line 10 speaks of things buried, but still alive. Thus, what appears to be dead and buried is still alive and about to be resurrected. The renewal of each day is also a reminder of the resurrection. Lines 11 and 12 might also refer to the actual darkness that came after Christ's crucifixion, and the glory of Easter morning. When we take this into account after lines 1-8, the meaning of the whole poem is revealed.

2.
b. It is fall. Unleaving means that the leaves are falling.

c. Fall is a traditional symbol for someone or something dying, as the leaves do at this time of year. The little girl does not really understand such things yet. To her, death is an abstraction, but she is still sad.

d. As Margaret grows older, her understanding of worldly things will increase as she gains mental maturity and experience. We need to read more to find out why she will weep.

e. This is the wellspring, or origin of sorrow, which is continually flowing.

f. Margaret's spirit understands something that she doesn't.

g. The origin of sorrow is the fall of Adam and Eve. This is what the poem is really about. Margaret does not understand the natural death she is headed for, nor the spiritual death she was born into. Her spirit, however, understands such things.

3.
e. The narrator is looking at the late sunset. It is winter and all branches are bare. The scene is melancholy to him.

f. The "Century's corpse" is the end, or expiration, of the century. The narrator compares it to the natural surroundings, which he describes as bleak and harsh. He obviously does not expect any spiritually uplifting event at the turn of the century.

g. It represents a voice of hope in the gloom.

h. The thrush waits until dark to sing. The darkness suggests spiritual darkness, which was more and more a concern of late Victorian society. The thrush cannot be seen, but its song can be heard. The romantic poets, like Shelley, would have said that the song represents a manifestation of a spirit. In this case, Hardy would probably want you to think of the spirit of God piercing the spiritual darkness. Typical of Hardy's pessimism, note that the narrator is "unaware" of any hope this might bring.

4.

c. This refers to the advances of science and technology, and theories like evolution, which greatly challenged the Bible and the heritage of our faith.

d. I don't think so, especially since the narrator of "The Oxen" hopes to see the animals kneeling. I think Hardy wanted desperately to believe.

e. Answers may vary.

5.

b. Being a creature of nature, it is indifferent to human endeavors.

c. This is Hardy's universal mind,` which shapes and drives nature.

d. It seems to have a sinister intent in this poem, as if it had a will to do harm.

e. Throughout the poem, the *Titanic* is a monstrous extravagance. Hardy would have us consider that the *Titanic* was out of tune with human decency and with nature, bringing disaster on itself.

# The Time Machine

**Teacher's Note: The beginning of this lesson includes a summary of the novel. This is designed to help you discuss the novel with the student. Also, some students are better able to understand the novel if they read a summary; however, it should not replace reading the full novel. Please note that any surprise element or suspense is revealed in the summary. Use the summary to best meet your student's needs.**

Lessons 31-32 Novel Unit–*The Time Machine* by H.G. Wells

Lesson 31

1. a. From 1880 to 1918, Western civilization continued the process of leaving traditions behind but fearing to let go of them. Although Marx and Engels had but a few followers in England, their works created a sense of alarm, as if such ideas could create cracks in the foundation of society. Freud, moreover, made people wonder if one's mind were subject to forces in the subconsciousness that could not be controlled by reason. Perhaps reality could be a matter of one's perception rather than a precise logical view that must be the same for everyone, like a mathematical formula. Einstein reinforced the understanding that reality is not a constant, as we had always believed. Things that we thought were unchangeable, such as the mass of an object, or time, were actually variable, depending on circumstances. Such things as these continued to erode traditional values. Moreover, improving technology continued to give men a sense of ordering out their environment without the help of traditional ways, values, and without much help from God. The changes in society created a strain on traditional literary conventions. Writers began to challenge the commonly upheld practices in form and content. Thus, we see the trends of breaking away from old forms, expanding subject matter, and, in poetry especially, expanding word usage. By 1880, two opposing views of art had emerged. One side held the traditional view that art was meant to comment on and improve society. The other side felt that art should have no restrictions except to express the artist's personal inclinations, which might or might not include opinions about society. Thus, art for society's sake, which is represented by Dickens' *A Tale of Two Cities*, was challenged by those who favored art for art's sake. Art for art's sake, of course, allowed the artist great freedom of expression. In England, the art for art's sake group tended to extremes. However, there were a good many talented writers who were less than extreme. Making slight departures from tradition, they made themselves acceptable. Thus, they were able to bring about change in a way that was noticeable, but not offensive. When H. G. Wells published his novella, *The Time Machine*, in 1895, the

world was ready for it. There had been enough scientific and technological advances to make the idea of time travel remotely believable. Furthermore, the artists'expanded freedom in subject matter allowed Wells to address the theory of evolution without fear of public retaliation.

b. Link to the Author: H.G. Wells

Herbert George Wells, writer, historian and philosopher, was born in 1866 in Bromley, England. An avid reader as a youngster, he earned a scholarship to the Normal School of Science, where he was deeply influenced by biologist and surgeon, Thomas Huxley (grandfather of Aldous Huxley). Wells questioned the fate of modern society with its technological and scientific advances. He was concerned that these advances outpaced man's intellectual development. For a short while, he joined the Fabian Society, a group of peaceful, social activists seeking democratic reform. In his later years, Wells wrote more about women's rights, war, capitalism, etc. *The Time Machine* (1895) was his first major work, thus bringing him much fame. Others are *The Island of Dr. Moreau* (1895), *The Invisible Man* (1897), and *The War of the Worlds* (1898). His well-known historical work is *The Outline of History* (1920). Wells died on August 13, 1946.

c. Summary of *The Time Machine*

The narrator and several educated friends discuss the possibility of time travel in the Time Traveller's (as he is called throughout the book) home. The Time Traveller, to prove his point that time as a fourth dimension can be travelled, brings out a little hand-held machine which he claims is a scale model of an actual time machine. After he turns on the machine and it disappears, he then takes the group to his laboratory where the full-sized time machine is almost complete. Everyone wonders how he made the model vanish and why he has made a full scale contraption.

A week later, the guests assemble for dinner again at the Time Traveller's house, but the Time Traveller is not there. As the guests sit down to eat, the Time Traveller appears, dirty and disheveled. The Time Traveller explains that he had travelled to the year 802,701 and begins to unravel his story.

In his journey into the future, he finds a primitive looking countryside, with only ruins of a greater society in evidence. Looking around, he sees a sphinx-like structure, which seems odd in a futuristic world. He soon discovers that the little people, called Eloi, are mentally on the level of about a five-year-old. These little people take him to a large, well-made, but disintegrating building. The Eloi eat only fruit, and the Time Traveller soon realizes that horses, cattle, etc. are now extinct. They speak no English which makes communication difficult.

When the Time Traveller discovers his time machine missing, he follows the drag marks on the ground to the spinx-like structure and enters in. There he discovers the underground world of the Morlocks, ape-like creatures that come out at night. The Morlocks live in complete darkness and have the ability to run machines.

The Time Traveller befriends Weena, an Eloi, when he saves her from drowning. She is like a child, always wanting to be by his side and very afraid of the dark. The Time Traveller soon discovers that the Morlocks actually tend to the needs of the Eloi like they were cattle. The Morlocks feed on the Eloi. Reflecting on his circumstances, he devises a plan to break into the sphinx and retrieve his time machine. He discovers a great building which turns out to be a huge museum. He regrets that evidence of a once great civilization has deteriorated so much and appears to be still declining. Surprisingly, he finds some well-preserved matches and a jar of camphor with which he makes a torch to fend off the Morlocks.

Leaving the museum too late, the Time Traveller, with Weena at his side, cannot make it to safety before dark. He builds a fire to keep the Morlocks away, then proceeds through the forest as a short cut to the sphinx. However, he is caught by the Morlocks. Although he is saved by the advancing fire which he started on the edge of the woods, little Weena is lost and presumed dead. As he returns to the sphinx, he finds the doors open and the time machine inside. Gleefully, he runs to the machine, but the doors close and the Morlocks attack him. He barely fends them off long enough to crank up the machine and escape.

Upon his return, no one believes his story. The next day, however, the narrator pays a visit to the Time Traveller, who is setting out again, this time with a backpack and a camera. The narrator watches as the Time Traveller and machine disappear, unfortunately, never to return.

d. Main characters in *The Time Machine*:

Time Traveller: the main character who invents and travels in the time machine
Eloi: child-like race of people
Morlocks: small, ape-like creatures with white skin and fur, and large eyes for seeing in the dark
Weena: a female Eloi whom the Time Traveller saves from drowning

e. Read Chapter 1.

f. How would the discussion about time strike Wells' readers in the year 1895?

2. a. Read Chapters 2-3.

b. What is the main conflict in the story?

c. What purposes do the characters have who surround the Time Traveller?

d. What new conflict has been added to the story in Chapter 3?

3. a. Read Chapter 4.

b. What are you reminded of by the sphinx-like statue and the building with the dining hall?

c. Could the little child-like people have built these structures?

d. What does this suggest?

e. How does the Time Traveller explain the state of civilization he sees in terms of civilization advancing?

4. a. Read Chapter 5.

   b. What are the physical attributes of the Morlocks?

   c. What does the Time Traveller conclude about the existence of the Morlocks and the Eloi?

   d. How does the Time Traveller explain the evolutionary process in reference to his own time?

   e. What mistake has he made regarding the relationship between the Eloi and the Morlocks?

   f. Has a new conflict been added to the story?

5. a. Read Chapters 6-7.

   b. What are some differences between the Morlocks and Eloi besides their physical features? Include differences in habitat.

   c. This time the Time Traveller figures out the relationship between the Morlocks and the Eloi. What is it?

   d. In what way is this world of the future a criticism of Wells' society?

1.

f. Such things were probably being discussed in scientific circles at the time. The novel plays upon a notion among many people that technology was capable of almost anything, making the story halfway believable.

2.

b. The main conflict is whether or not the Time Traveller is to be believed.

c. They serve as intelligent skeptics who ask pertinent questions and sometimes provide answers, much the way we would if we were present.

d. The Time Traveller does not know if he is in a hostile land or not. At this point, he does not know if he will return to his own time.

3.

b. We are reminded of the art and architecture of ancient Western civilizations, such as Greece and Egypt.

c. Not according to the information we've been given.

d. It shows that mankind attained a high level of civilization and then degenerated into these child-like people.

e. He sees the state of civilization as an evolutionary process. He thinks the little people are socially in harmony and have no need of the things we do, such as strong government, military protection, advanced technology, and medicine, etc. He thinks that he is viewing a sort of utopia in which the need to evolve forward has ceased.

4.

b. The Morlocks are small, ape-like creatures with white skin and fur, and large eyes for seeing in the dark.

c. He reasons that two races or species of man have evolved from his time.

d. He sees the division of Eloi and Morlocks as the evolutionary process of division between wealthy industrialists and laborers.

e. He reasons that the Eloi are descendants of England's wealthy ruling class, and he assumes that they are in control.

f. There are numerous suggestions that there is conflict between the Eloi and the Morlocks, which could be dangerous for the Time Traveller.

5.

b. The Morlocks apparently have no structure to live in–just tunnels and caverns, but these are of their own making. They are able to operate and perhaps to make their own machinery, whereas the Eloi apparently have no such aptitudes. The two societies have developed different languages. Unlike the Eloi, the Morlocks are carnivorous and hostile to the Time Traveller.

**They are unclean and gross, and their dark habitat seems to represent the dark side of human nature, whereas Eloi are rather innocent and good-natured.**

c. **The Eloi are tended by the Morlocks as a food supply.**

d. **Notice that the Time Traveller always refers to faults in his own society's time which give rise to what he finds in the future.**

1. a. Read Chapters 8-9 of H.G. Wells' *The Time Machine*.

   b. Why are the things in the museum so well-preserved?

   c. How does the loss of Weena affect the Time Traveller?

   d. How does the loss of Weena affect the Time Traveller's chances for escape?

2. a. Read the rest of *The Time Machine*.

   b. As the Time Traveller moves forward, what happens to the life forms on Earth?

   c. At what stage of this development does mankind, according to the Time Traveller, begin the process of devolution?

3. a. With your teacher's permission, watch the old, black and white film version of "The Time Machine," starring Rod Taylor.

   b. Discuss with your teacher your reaction to the movie compared to the novel.

4-5. Write a five hundred word essay (about two typewritten pages, double-spaced) about your reaction to the novel.

1.

b. They are well-preserved because microorganisms faded out of existence, slowing down the decaying process.

c. He feels the loss of companionship. The Eloi have the bright side of human traits, whereas the Morlocks have the darker side, and he responds to each accordingly.

d. On the one hand, he is free to act without any burden. However, if he tries to find her, he will be greatly hindered.

2.

b. They continue to devolve into simpler forms.

c. Having reached perfection, and without any challenges, mankind ceases to exercise brainpower and physical strength. Since there is no need for these things, they phase out.

# The Modern Poets

1. a. Modern Age

During the years from 1900 to the outbreak of World War I (1914), there was a growing distance between the traditionalists and the liberals. As is so often the case, liberals tended to have more influence on intellectuals, with many artists among their ranks. Liberal ideas were slow to filter down to the average person, who seldom even cared much about Darwin, Freud, or Einstein. Like most of us, the average Englishman needed something more tangible than a theory or two as evidence that he should abandon his traditions. This tangible evidence was provided by the brutal, grisly reality of World War I.

Most Englishmen expected the war to be over in a matter of months. The English felt that their superior way of life, which involved everything from economic and military to spiritual superiority, would quickly prevail. However, as the war progressed, and the number of English dead mounted without accomplishing any military impact to speak of, it became apparent to the soldiers that they were deceived. Made to fight by the traditional and obsolete strategies of warfare, which were obviously driving the men into senseless massacres, the soldiers lost faith in their traditional ways of life.

The English soldier was told to fight for God and country. As thousands of soldiers were ordered to senselessly charge enemy lines only to be slaughtered, the men began to realize the futility of what they were doing. However, the military leadership was slow to change, and stood by their traditions, backed by the authority of God and country. To the soldier, this represented church and state and all the values they upheld. Seeing that these values were responsible for so much meaningless loss of life, the men gave up on their traditions, and those who survived brought their sentiments back to England. Thus, the Modern Age, during which so many changes in lifestyles and attitudes developed, began after World War I.

By the end of World War I, all of Western civilization had become disillusioned. The scientific and technological advances that seemed so promising had been adapted to create destructive machines of war. Even the average person realized that Western civilization not only had the capacity, but the will to destroy itself. People were afraid and disgusted with a civilization that could take what should be meant for good and turn it against itself.

For the artist, the old forms and values were no longer appropriate. For the poet, he needed freedom to express his feelings about the repulsive things he saw in his world. The poet no longer felt restrained by having to focus on the uplifting and inspirational. It was time, now, to say what needed to be said, regardless of the traditions of the past.

b. Poet's Corner

**Thomas Stearns Eliot**, poet and playwright, was born in St.Louis, Missouri, on September 26, 1888. He was born into a prominent family, the son of a businessman and a poet. He studied at Harvard, the Sorbonne, and Oxford University. He moved to London in 1915, and there, met the poet, Ezra Pound, who encouraged him in his writing. He became a British citizen in 1927 and died on January 4, 1965.

c. It was time for a poet of great talent to arrive and give validation to the new ways. In 1922, T.S. Eliot published his poem, "The Waste Land," all about Western civilization, paving the way for the Modern Era in poetry. Never before had anyone dared to make a panoramic criticism of society. After World War I, however, no one could argue the point. As for the poem's diction, it ranges from the extremely erudite to the extremely colloquial, all of which is done so artistically that every word is carefully placed, yet the tone is conversational. The form, free verse, was chosen by Eliot because he felt that the old forms, representing old values, were no longer appropriate for the Modern Era.

It was said that the influence of Eliot was so powerful that subsequent poets were bound to follow his example. This is not entirely true. It is more accurate to say that subsequent poets had the freedom to choose the subject matter, diction, and form that they felt was best for their poetry.

Although Eliot was an American, he lived in England for years. Understandably, his influence extended over British poets as much as Americans.

d. Read Part I of "The Waste Land," titled "The Burial of the Dead."

April is the cruellest month, breeding
Lilacs out of the dead land, mixing
Memory and desire, stirring
Dull roots with spring rain.
Winter kept us warm, covering
Earth in forgetful snow, feeding
A little life with dried tubers.
Summer surprised us, coming over the Starnbergersee
With a shower of rain, we stopped in the colonnade,
And went on in sunlight, into the Hofgarten,
And drank coffee, and talked for an hour.
12 Bin gar keine Russin, stamm' aus Litauen, echt deutsch.
And when we were children, staying at the archduke's,
My cousin's, he took me out on a sled,
And I was frightened. He said, Marie,
Marie, hold on tight. And down we went.
In the mountains, there you feel free.
18 I read, much of the night, and go south in the winter.

What are the roots that clutch, what branches grow
20 Out of this stony rubbish? Son of man,
You cannot say, or guess, for you know only
A heap of broken images, where the sun beats,
23 And the dead tree gives no shelter, the cricket no relief,
And the dry stone no sound of water. Only
There is shadow under this red rock,
(Come in under the shadow of this red rock),
And I will show you something different from either
Your shadow at morning striding behind you
Or your shadow at evening rising to meet you;
30 I will show you fear in a handful of dust.

31 Frisch weht der Wind
Der Heimat zu.
Mein Irisch Kind,
Wo weilest du?

'You gave me hyacinths first a year ago;
'they called me the hyacinth girl.'
–Yet when we came back, late, from the Hyacinth garden,
Your arms full, and your hair wet, I could not
Speak, and my eyes failed, I was neither
Living nor dead, and I knew nothing,
Looking into the heart of light, the silence.
42 Oed' und leer das Meer.

43 Madame Sosostris, famous clairvoyante,
Had a bad cold, nevertheless
Is known to be the wisest woman in Europe,
46 With a wicked pack of cards. Here, said she,
Is your card, the drowned Phoenician Sailor.
(Those are pearls that were his eyes. Look!)
Here is Belladonna, the Lady of the Rocks,
The lady of situations.
Here is the man with three staves, and here the Wheel,
And here is the one-eyed merchant, and this card,
Which is blank, is something he carries on his back,
Which I am forbidden to see. I do not find
55 The Hanged Man. Fear death by water.
I see crowds of people, walking round in a ring.
Thank you. If you see dear Mrs. Equitone,
Tell her I bring the horoscope myself:
One must be so careful these days.

60 Unreal City,
Under the brown fog of a winter dawn,
A crowd flowed over London Bridge, so many,
63 I had not thought death had undone so many.
64 Sighs, short and infrequent, were exhaled,
And each man fixed his eyes before his feet.
Flowed up the hill and down King William Street,
To where Saint Mary Woolnoth kept the hours
68 With a dead sound on the final stroke of nine.
69 There I saw one I knew, and stopped him, crying: 'Stetson!
'You who were with me in the ships at Mylae!
'That corpse you planted last year in your garden,
'Has it begun to sprout? Will it bloom this year?
'Or has the sudden frost disturbed its bed?
'Oh keep the Dog far hence, that's friend to men,
'Or with his nails he'll dig it up again!
76 'You! hypocrite lecteur!–mon semblable,–mon frère!'

e. Line 12 translates:
   I am not Russian at all; I come from Lithuania,
   I am a real German.

   Lines 31-34 translates:
   The wind blows fresh
   To the Homeland
   My Irish Girl
   Where are you lingering?

   Line 42 translates:
   Desolate and empty the sea

   Line 76 translates:
   You, Hypocrite reader! - my doppelganger - my brother!

f. Begin writing poetry today. Try using free verse. Work on your poem throughout the week.

2. a. Poet's Corner

   **Wilfred Owen** was born in Owestry, U.K., on March 18, 1893. Born into an evangelical Anglican home, he was the eldest of four children. Fighting in World War I impacted his life greatly. During the war, he was hospitalized for neurasthenia (shell shock), and there met poet Siegfried Sassoon. Upon Sassoon's urging and inspiration, Owen wrote most of his famous poems during this time. He later returned to the front line and was killed on November 4, 1918, seven days before Armistice.

   b. Wilfred Owen was one of a number of poets who wrote about World War I. Owen was actually at the notorious Battle of Somme, about which a great deal has been written. Therefore, Owen, an infantryman, witnessed some of the grisliest moments of World War I. His poems about such experiences are powerfully evocative and relate the struggles of the mind and body common to an infantryman of any war.

   c. In order to see more clearly the contrast between the Victorian mentality and the Modern period, read Tennyson's "The Charge of the Light Brigade." Tennyson read an account of it in the newspaper. The order for the men to charge was due to confusion on the commander's part. About three fourths of the six hundred men died in the misguided attack.

d. Read Tennyson's "The Charge of the Light Brigade."

1 Half a league, half a league,
Half a league onward,
All in the valley of Death
Rode the six hundred.
5 "Forward, the Light Brigade!
Charge for the guns!" he said:
Into the valley of Death
Rode the six hundred.

"Forward, the Light Brigade!"
10 Was there a man dismay'd?
Not tho' the soldier knew
Someone had blunder'd:
Theirs not to make reply,
Theirs not to reason why,
15 Theirs but to do and die:
Into the valley of Death
Rode the six hundred.

Cannon to right of them,
Cannon to left of them,
20 Cannon in front of them
Volley'd and thunder'd;
Storm'd at with shot and shell,
Boldly they rode and well,
Into the jaws of Death,
25 Into the mouth of Hell
Rode the six hundred.

Flash'd all their sabres bare,
Flash'd as they turn'd in air,
Sabring the gunners there,
30 Charging an army, while
All the world wonder'd:
Plunged in the battery-smoke
Right thro' the line they broke;

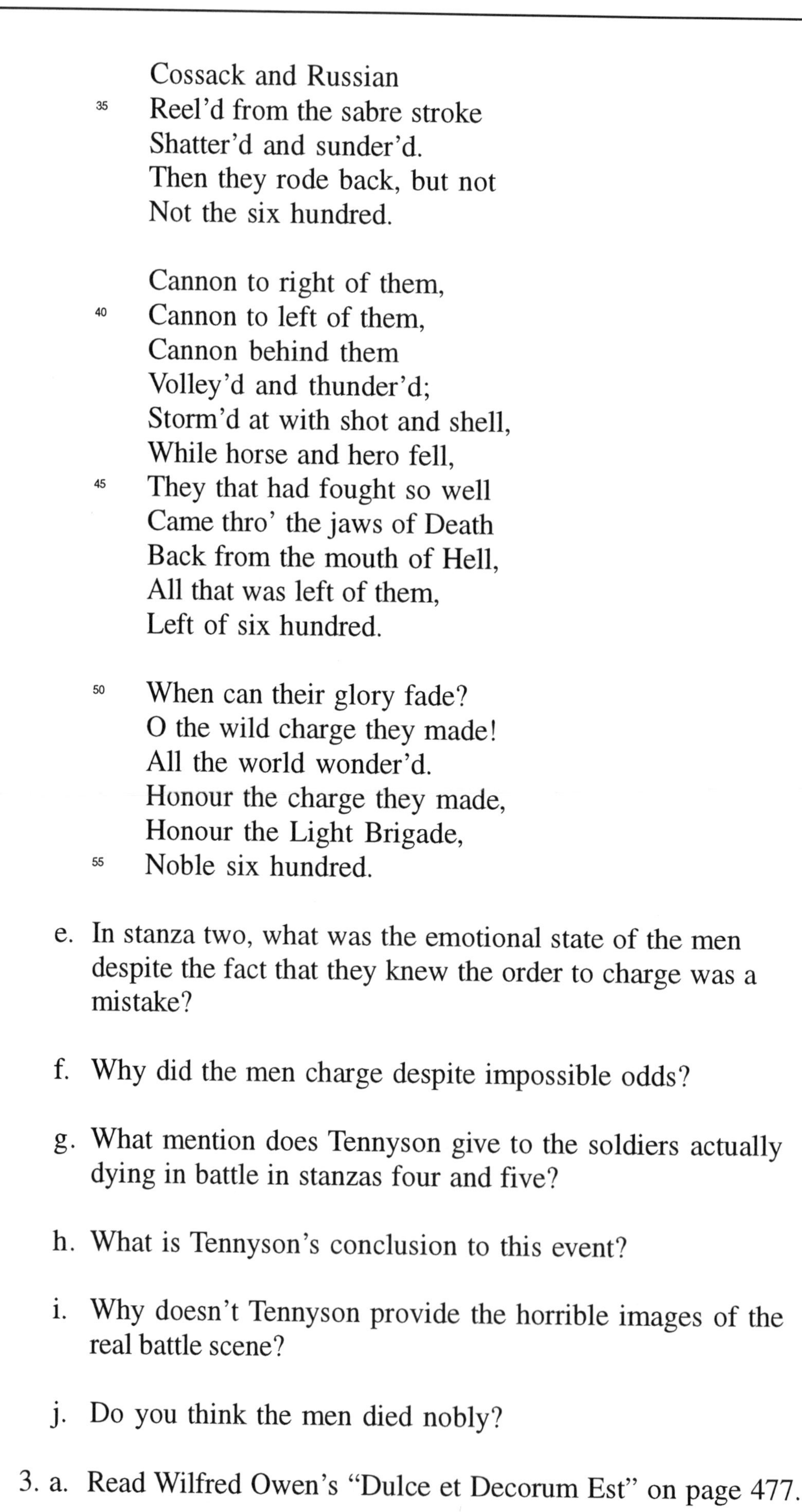

Cossack and Russian
35 Reel'd from the sabre stroke
Shatter'd and sunder'd.
Then they rode back, but not
Not the six hundred.

Cannon to right of them,
40 Cannon to left of them,
Cannon behind them
Volley'd and thunder'd;
Storm'd at with shot and shell,
While horse and hero fell,
45 They that had fought so well
Came thro' the jaws of Death
Back from the mouth of Hell,
All that was left of them,
Left of six hundred.

50 When can their glory fade?
O the wild charge they made!
All the world wonder'd.
Honour the charge they made,
Honour the Light Brigade,
55 Noble six hundred.

e. In stanza two, what was the emotional state of the men despite the fact that they knew the order to charge was a mistake?

f. Why did the men charge despite impossible odds?

g. What mention does Tennyson give to the soldiers actually dying in battle in stanzas four and five?

h. What is Tennyson's conclusion to this event?

i. Why doesn't Tennyson provide the horrible images of the real battle scene?

j. Do you think the men died nobly?

3. a. Read Wilfred Owen's "Dulce et Decorum Est" on page 477.

Note: "Dulce et decorum est pro patria mori" is from Horace, *Odes III*. It means "Sweet and fitting it is to die for the fatherland."

b. In stanza one what impressions do the images of the soldiers make on you in stanza one?

c. How does the transition from lines 8-9 emphasize the struggles of the soldiers?

d. Why does Owen go into rather lengthy detail to describe the dying soldier?

e. The changes in values are evident from Tennyson to Owen. Do you completely agree with Owen?

4. a. Poet's Corner

**Robert Graves** was born in Wimbledon, England, on July 24, 1895. He was one of ten children and was influenced by his father's love for Celtic poetry and his mother's faith. Graves also served in World War I, but survived it. He, too, was struck by the vast differences between what he was told at home and what he saw on the battlefield. Although his poetry reflects this conflict, Graves put these things behind him and matured as a poet. Graves is primarily known for his historical novels, like *I, Claudius*, but he always considered himself a poet first. He lived to be ninety years old and died in 1985.

b. The effects of breaking with tradition are seen in Graves' poetry through his theories of poetry. Having been influenced by Freudian psychology, Graves developed a theory of poetry as a way of expressing suppressed inner conflicts. As his experiences from the war became more distant however, Graves began to reevaluate his theory. He developed the idea that poetry derives from a source outside the poet, as if the mythological Muse really did exist. This is consistent with the disillusionment in which any understanding of God's creation and His giving of gifts to individuals is not present.

c. Read "Rocky Acres," page 489.

d. What is the main point of the first three stanzas?

e. If you have not already done so, look up any unfamiliar words in the last stanza.

How do you interpret the last stanza?

5. a. Read "Recalling War," pp. 496- 497.

b. In stanza one, why do the disabled "forget" their disabilities for a moment?

c. What is the attitude toward the coming war in stanza two?

d. What is meant by the last three lines of the poem?

e. Why does Owen's poem recall the horrors of war better than Graves' poem?

2.

e. According to the poem, the men are undismayed.

f. They were good soldiers who took orders without questioning them.

g. Stanza four says the British broke the Russian line and the Russian soldiers were dealt heavy losses. In stanza five, the British are spoken of as "heroes" that "fall."

h. The men who died were courageous and noble. They should be honored for obeying orders even though it meant death.

i. To show the men being slaughtered and cut to pieces was all but unthinkable for poetry at the time. It would have dishonored those who died.

j. Answers may vary. From our present day viewpoint, it was senseless waste that would be condemned by everyone. In Tennyson's time, the men died heroically.

3.

b. These are infantrymen who have been in battle a long time. Their bodies, minds, and equipment have all been severely tested. This is the reality of war.

c. The men are weary to the point of collapse. In this condition, they face a vicious attack to which they must react quickly and alertly. It is almost too much to bear, but that's war.

d. To emphasize the reality of the horrors of war, Owen singles out this incident, because to die this way could not be much worse.

e. Answers may vary, but the following contains my thoughts. Owen is right to point out that many men die needlessly in war. However, he went too far, even by today's standards. We live freely in the United States because of the thousands and thousands who died to keep us free. Even though the English wasted countless lives upholding traditional methods and values for warfare, England was kept free by those who paid the price.

4.

d. Graves gives a description of his home and surrounding land. It is a harsh country, but Graves is obviously very fond of it.

e. Graves glorifies the land by saying that it had an honored place after the Flood. However, he claims that demigods roam there, giving a mythological, rather than a Biblical glorification to the area. His point is to give the place special recognition.

5.

b. Although their wounds are still with them, they have put the war behind them and moved on.

c. In our day, we call this trash talking. The poet reveals the overconfidence the English felt before they went to war.

d. **The poet seems to think that the lessons of World War I will be forgotten, and that pride and a fall are bound to be repeated.**

e. **Owen chooses a specific, detailed incident, whereas Graves makes only general statements. Graves' purpose is to show distance from the war, so his method is consistent with his purpose.**

# Animal Farm

**Teacher's Note: The beginning of this lesson includes a summary of the novel. This is designed to help you discuss the novel with the student. Also, some students are better able to understand the novel if they read a summary; however, it should not replace reading the full novel. Please note that any surprise element or suspense is revealed in the summary. Use the summary to best meet your student's needs.**

Lessons 34-36 Novel Unit - *Animal Farm* by George Orwell (any unabridged publication)

Lesson 34

1. a. Link to the Author: George Orwell

Eric Blair, better known by his pen name, George Orwell, was born in 1903 in India (part of the British Empire at the time). During his school years in England, he was often shunned and persecuted by his wealthier, class-conscious teachers and classmates for his lower class status. After completing Eton College, he joined the Imperial Police (then British ruled) in Burma. There again, he witnessed inequality and oppression, but from an angle with him on top. Returning to Paris and London, he worked meager jobs and lived in relative poverty. Out of his experiences of social injustice, he wrote his first novels. Orwell promoted democratic socialism and claimed to be pro-socialist, he was against capitalism and communism. He believed that wealth should be distributed and class distinctions diminished or eliminated. The original ideals of Marx and Engels appealed to Orwell, but he saw them as perverted, especially under Stalin. Orwell fought for the Republic during the Spanish Civil War, was shot in the throat and returned to England. He died in 1950 from tuberculosis.

b. Summary of *Animal Farm*

Mr. Jones, the owner of Manor Farm, drinks too much, often neglects to feed the animals, and carries a whip. Old Major, the farmer's prize boar, tells the animals that Man is evil and that all their hardships are due to these two-legged creatures. He is the visionary who draws a utopian picture of plenty and peace for the animals—a life free from the dominion of Man. He encourages a Rebellion but soon after dies, leaving Snowball and Napoleon, also pigs, to lead the animals. Sheer hunger initiates and drives the Rebellion, and Mr. and Mrs. Jones are chased out of their farm. The farm is renamed Animal Farm. Soon after the Rebellion, the pigs teach themselves to read and write and a list of Seven Commandments appear on the barn wall. One by one, the commandments are broken by the pigs, but the other animals are lulled into believing lies and disinformation spread successfully by Squealer. The other animals are not as smart as the pigs and are easily led. Snowball and Napoleon keep the milk and apples for themselves with Squealer convincing the others that they are the hardest workers and need this extra food. At any hint of discontentment, Squealer conjures up the other animals' greatest fears, by asking, "Do you want Jones back as your master?" This squelches the other animals' doubts every time. Snowball and Napoleon often quarrel, finally leading Napoleon to oust Snowball, his competitor. Napoleon orders the continued building of the windmill, Snowball's original idea to bring ease into the animals' lives. Napoleon's selfish motive brings hardship to all the workers. Eventually, Boxer, the loyal workhorse, dies giving his life for (apparently) nothing. Even in death, Boxer is used to further Napoleon's selfish ends. By now, the Seven Commandments have been reduced to "All animals are equal, but some animals are more equal than others." What began as a way to free themselves from Man's oppression has quickly turned full circle. By the end of the novel, the pigs have broken all the commandments. They are sleeping in beds, wearing clothes, killing other animals, drinking alcohol, consorting with Men, and walking on two legs. The other animals find that it is now impossible to distinguish the pigs from Man.

Note: George Orwell's *Animal Farm*, published in 1945, was written as a criticism of Soviet Russian Communism under Stalin. Although the novel attacks Stalinist Russia, it really is about any authoritarian government, and is as applicable today as it was then. The book's main character, Napoleon, represents Stalin, whom Orwell regarded as a traitor to his own country and an enemy of socialism.

c. Major characters in *Animal Farm*:

Old Major: the old boar, a visionary, who calls for a better life and Rebellion

Snowball: the prize boar who competes for leadership of Animal Farm

Napoleon: the ambitious, young boar who becomes the leader

Boxer: the work horse, the unquestioning hard worker

Benjamin: the donkey, a skeptic
Moses: the raven, Mr. Jones' pet, who tells stories of Sugarcandy Mountain
Squealer: the pig who excuses the actions of the boars with lies
Mr. Jones: the master of Manor Farm, who whips and neglects the animals

d. Read Chapter 1 of *Animal Farm.*

e. Old Major calls the other animals comrades. He also reminds them that they are the working class and are exploited by the privileged men. What does this remind you of?

f. Is Old Major's assertion that all men are enemies correct?

g. Is it true that "all the evils of this life of ours [the animals] spring from the tyranny of human beings"?

h. There is evidence in Chapter 1 that all animals are not necessarily comrades. What shows us this?

i. Which animals were called the "clever ones"?

2. a. Read Chapter 2.

b. With regard to the preparation for the rebellion and the rebellion itself, what are you reminded of that we have already read in another novel?

c. Each kind of animal represents a certain segment of society. What does Moses represent?

d. Mollie's questions are called the "stupidest of all." However, what is revealed by the answers to Mollie's questions?

e. Commandments one and seven have already failed. What evidence do we have that the animals do not uphold commandment number two?

f. How do commandments three through five threaten rather than create an ideal state?

g. What evidence do we have that Napoleon has his own interests at heart?

3. a. Read Chapters 3-4.

   b. Chapter 3 challenges one of the seven commandments. Which commandment is being challenged, and what is the point?

   c. How do the pigs violate commandment seven?

   d. Who emerges as the leader of Animal Farm after the Battle of the Cowshed?

4. a. Read Chapter 5.

   b. Why does Mollie leave the farm?

   c. What are Napoleon's three sources of power?

   d. In terms of their attitudes toward community welfare, what is the difference between Napoleon and Snowball?

5. a. Read Chapter 6.

   b. The destruction of the windmill actually helps Napoleon's interests. How?

   c. How does Napoleon use Snowball to his advantage?

   d. What is the main point of Chapter 6?

1.
e. It reminds one of communism.

f. No. Examples to the contrary are too numerous to list.

g. If Orwell attributes human intelligence and reason to the animals, then the animals are subject to human-like shortcomings that create their own root problems.

h. The rats are allowed to be called comrades only by a vote. Even at that, there were abstentions.

i. The pigs and dogs were called the "clever ones."

2.
b. Defarge's revolutionary preparation and then the storming of the Bastille followed a similar pattern. (*A Tale of Two Cities*)

c. Moses represents organized religion.

d. The animals will be denied material things that they had under man's rule. Also, animals will be denied certain freedoms. Mollie should have the right to wear her ribbons, but she will be forced not to.

e. The pigs regard Moses as a spy and talebearer, which makes him an enemy.

f. These commandments deny freedoms that some animals might like to have. These commandments could be amended to deny further freedoms.

g. Napoleon sends the other animals away while he takes care of the milk, which disappears without being accounted for.

3.
b. Commandment seven. There are great differences among the animals intellectually, physically, and behaviorally.

c. The pigs demand special privileges for their special abilities.

d. Snowball emerges as the leader.

4.
b. She is unhappy that she is denied things she likes. Furthermore, she does not like the regimen that has been prescribed for her. She would rather work for some human in return for the lifestyle she wants.

c. Napoleon gained a following by criticizing Snowball behind his back once debates were over. Another source of power, of course, is force. Thirdly, he controls with propaganda and threats.

d. Snowball is genuinely interested in bettering the lives of the other animals. Napoleon wants to use the community to serve his own interests.

5.
b. The labor necessary to build the windmill keeps the animals busy and tired. They hardly have any time or energy to object to the changes that have come about.

c. **Snowball is a scapegoat. Problems that arise can be blamed on him directly, or indirectly, by creating lies about Snowball's misguided notions of the past.**

d. **Many of the seven commandments and resolutions have been broken by the elite class of pigs. The pigs are manipulating the system to create more privileges for themselves.**

1. a. Read Chapter 7 of George Orwell's *Animal Farm.*

   b. Why does Napoleon have to create the Snowball sabotage stories regarding the farm's productivity?

   c. Identify one way that the Snowball's sabotage stories backfire on the administration.

   d. Why does Napoleon make some of the animals confess to crimes against Animal Farm?

   e. Why was Boxer attacked by the dogs?

   f. What four things does Clover resolve to do in order to escape the fate of those who were executed?

2. a. Read Chapter 8.

   b. In the beginning of the chapter, what happens to Napoleon's image as he isolates himself and lets others take care of the public relations?

   c. What advantage is there to the pigs to make Frederick a powerful adversary?

   d. How do the pigs feel after the Battle of the Windmill?

   e. How do the rest of the animals feel?

   f. Most of the animals do not see through the pigs' treachery. What three main methods of control do the pigs use to subjugate the rest of the animals?

3. a. Read Chapter 9.

   b. Napoleon declares the Spontaneous Demonstrations to celebrate the struggles and triumphs of Animal Farm. What is their real purpose?

   c. Why is Moses tolerated?

   d. Why don't the pigs try to save Boxer's life?

e. Is there any difference between what Napoleon did to Boxer and what Jones would have done?

4. a. Read Chapter 10.

   b. We see that the pigs have become just like the humans. What does this show us about the social structure of Animal Farm?

   c. What is Orwell trying to say about human nature by drawing the similarities between pigs and humans?

   d. What does the scene in the farmhouse involving the pigs and humans suggest about relationships between Soviet Russia and the West?

   e. Are the animals better off under Napoleon or were they better off under Jones?

5. Today, begin a book report on *Animal Farm*. You will have all of next week to complete your assignment. (Refer to Lesson 29 on how to write a book review.)

1.
b. It is the administration's fault that things are as bad as they are. Napoleon needs a believable lie to take the blame away from himself and put it elsewhere.

c. The other animals use them to excuse their own mistakes and failures.

d. Almost all the animals who confessed were in some degree resisting the authority Napoleon had established. Napoleon is eliminating any possible threat to his empire.

e. At first, Boxer refused to believe that Snowball had been fighting on the side of the enemy at the Battle of the Cowhed, and this was apparently reported back to Napoleon.

f.
1) Be faithful
2) Work hard
3) Carry out her orders
4) Accept Napoleon's leadership

2.
b. Napoleon is becoming god-like, as if he, and not God, were able to watch over everything and provide for all.

c. It gives the animals a reason to work together to preserve and defend Animal Farm. The sacrifices necessary to do this seem reasonable to prevent a Frederick takeover.

d. They feel victorious and show it by celebrating.

e. Boxer probably sums it up best. He asks what victory has been achieved, and he feels a sense of despair as he looks ahead to the life that he must now face.

f. The first two ways are contained in the propaganda that the pigs promote. First, the propaganda is full of lies. However, it is also necessary to have a certain amount of truth to manipulate the others. If this does not work, then there is the threat of brutality and death.

3.
b. Their real purpose is to distract the animals from thinking about how difficult their lives really are.

c. Marx said that religion is the opiate of the people. Moses helps keep the animals pacified by offering comfort in very difficult circumstances. He actually helps the pigs, since he is no threat to their rule.

d. The expense of making him well is greater than his usefulness to the farm. Boxer is useful only in terms of the money he can bring from the horse slaughterer.

e. There is very little difference, if any. This is one of the points of the episode.

4.
b. The pigs have created an elite group which separates itself

**from the others more and more as time goes on.**

c. **Pigs have a reputation for self-indulgence. It is often said that pigs become sloppy, fat, and mean if they are left to be themselves with no restraints. Orwell seems to suggest that the same is true of people.**

d. **Soviet Russia wanted desperately to be equal to or above Western civilization, and to be accepted on equal terms. Although the two sides had limited cooperation with each other, neither side could ever trust each other, as the card game shows.**

e. **Perhaps they would have had slightly more food and rest under Jones, but their fates would have been just about the same.**

Lesson 36

You will spend this week working on the book review on George Orwell's *Animal Farm*. Refer to Lesson 29 on how to write a book review.

# *Book Review Assessment II*

To help you assess your student's book review, complete the following checklist.

The book review contains:

1) title, author, publisher, place and date of publication ______________

2) brief overview of the book in the opening paragraph ______________

3) a summary of the story, including information identifying the characters ______________

4) an explanation of the major themes, complete with examples or quotations ______________

5) the student's opinion of the book, including his reasons ______________

6) correct grammar, punctuation, and spelling ______________

If your student has missed any of the above points, encourage him to go back and improve his book review. Congratulate him for his effort and completion.

# Literary Terms

**abstract** - referring to an idea that cannot be grasped
**archaism**- the use of words no longer commonly used
**blank verse** - unrhymed iambic pentameter
**Classical sonnet** - a sonnet with a rhyme scheme **abbaabba** in the octave and either **ccdcdd** or **cdecde** in the sestet; also called Petrarchan sonnet
**closed couplet** - poetry consisting of two lines of rhymed iambic pentameter, having a slight pause after the first line, a heavy pause, or stop, after the second line
**commentary** - what occurs when a narrator interprets his experience by making observations or conclusions
**concrete** - referring to an object that can be grasped by one of the senses
**couplet** - two consecutive lines of poetry usually having rhyme and meter
**dialect** - a form of speech spoken by a definable group of people
**diction** - the choice of words, phrases, or sentence structure
**dramatization** - technique used when a character is placed in a situation and relates what happens from his point of view as the scene unfolds
**enjambment** - in poetry, when one line ends without a pause and continues into the next line; also called a run-on
**free verse** - poetry consisting of no particular pattern of rhyme, meter, or form
**heroic couplet** - same as closed couplet
**iamb** - an unstressed syllable followed by a stressed syllable
**iambic pentameter** - poetry consisting of five iambic feet per line
**image** - a word or phrase that brings a mental picture of the senses to mind
**line** - in poetry, a sequence of words written as a separate entity
**metaphor** - a figure of speech that compares two unlike things without the words *like* or *as*
**meter** - the rhythmic pattern of stressed and unstressed syllables
**octave**- an eight line stanza, usually within a sonnet
**onomatopoeia** - a word that conveys how a word sounds i.e. slam, buzz
**personification** - a figure of speech in which human characteristics are attributed to non-human things
**Petrarchan sonnet** - a sonnet with a rhyme scheme **abbaabba** in the octave and either **cdcdcd** or **cdecde** in the sestet; also called Classical sonnet
**primitivism** - a belief that man is basically good but society has made him evil; by returning to God, man could to be restored to God
**quatrain** - a four line stanza
**rhyme** - the repetition of similar sounding syllables usually at the end of lines
**romanticism** - state of the arts that went beyond reason, emphasizing the spiritual and emotional
**run-on** - in poetry, when one line ends without a pause and continues into the next line; also called enjambment
**sentimentalism** - technique to arouse emotion that exceeds the norm, usually in sympathy, sorrow, etc.